Edward.Henry Knight

A Study of the savage Weapons at the Centennial Exhibition,

Philadelphia, 1876

Edward.Henry Knight

A Study of the savage Weapons at the Centennial Exhibition, Philadelphia, 1876

ISBN/EAN: 9783743358805

Manufactured in Europe, USA, Canada, Australia, Japa

Cover: Foto ©ninafisch / pixelio.de

Manufactured and distributed by brebook publishing software
(www.brebook.com)

Edward.Henry Knight

A Study of the savage Weapons at the Centennial Exhibition,

Philadelphia, 1876

GENERAL APPENDIX

TO THE

SMITHSONIAN REPORT FOR 1879.

The object of this appendix is to illustrate the operations of the Institution, as well as to furnish information of a character suited especially to its correspondents and collaborators.

A STUDY OF THE SAVAGE WEAPONS AT THE CENTENNIAL EXHIBITION, PHILADELPHIA, 1876

By Edward H. Knight, A. M., LL. D.

INTRODUCTION.

The objects illustrated in the following paper are merely those of one class, shown at the Centennial Exhibition, in Philadelphia, 1876.

The paper, therefore, makes no pretense to completeness, as the weapons shown in the various national sections were in most cases treated as mere casual objects thrown in as curiosities, and in many cases so little esteemed by the parties in charge that they were huddled away under tables; surprise was sometimes expressed that any one should pore over the coarse and clumsy when the best talent of the country had exerted itself on the objects prominently displayed as worthy of notice.

More than 700 sketches of the crude and curious implements shown at the exhibition were made by the author; the following were a portion, including weapons only, while a much larger, embracing tools of industry, were the subject of a series of papers in the Atlantic Monthly, May, 1877, to April, 1878, inclusive.

There was no concurrence of design in the exhibition, so far as concerns our present subject. In almost all cases the objects were mere casual additions; in a few the scientific spirit was evident, and some care had been taken to illustrate this side of ethnology.

To illustrate: The curious collection of musical instruments and weapons brought by Capt. Long (Bey) from Central Africa was almost hidden in a corner, while the tufted carpets, embroidered robes, and horse-trappings were prominently shown. In the collection from Java and the other Dutch Colonies in the Malay seas, much more was shown of the appliances of the semi-savage races of the region. Brazil, which had so admirable a collection of its agricultural and forest products, had scarcely anything which touches our subject, and Japan had a great deal, though much less in the way of its weapons than in its industries and domestic implements.

The Centennial Exhibition was mainly of the means and results of modern industry and art, and the primitive objects were comparatively but strays and occasionals. It is, therefore, not the author's fault that the exhibit of the relatively rude is so incomplete, as he has rigidly confined his illustrations to objects actually exhibited there; and he is not responsible for the circumstance that the comparatively unknown and little thought of Portuguese colony of Angola had more in his line of search than the whole continent of South America.

It may be mentioned, however, that the Dutch and Portuguese colonies had a manifold better exhibit in Paris in 1878, and that the former had the finest ethnological display of the mechanical ingenuity of an unlettered people which it has ever been the good fortune of the author to see.

Types of Savage Weapons.—The simplest form of a weapon is a stick; a heavy stick is a club. The club with a knob becomes a mace; the swelling end sharpened on one edge is an axe. Point the stick and it is a spear; if light, it is a javelin; shorter still, it is a dagger for close quarters. Flatten the stick and give it an edge, it becomes a sword; or, if short, it is a knife.

So far the weapon is a single piece of wood; but some ingenious man contrives to mount a stone in a withe, or sling it with a thong or in the skin of an animal's leg, or lash it to a stick; or he learns how to project a light spear from a bow, or a heavier one by means of a stick or a thong. We find all these modifications in the collections from various countries at the Centennial.

Another type of weapon is the stone or club which is thrown; the simplest method is, of course, the mere hurling of stones by the hand. Then there are several forms of slings; the one having two thongs and a pocket, and the other a stick for hurling a perforated stone. The stone on the end of a string may be considered a third kind, and out of this grows the *bolas*—several associated balls on as many strings—which has a whirling motion when thrown. All of these also were exhibited. The lasso of South America naturally occurs to one in speaking of the *bolas*, though the noosed lasso belongs to another class of devices, not exactly a weapon but a snare.

Materials employed.—The statement of Lucretius (*De rerum naturæ*) in regard to the discovery of weapons relates rather to the material than the form. "The first weapons of mankind were the hands, nails, and teeth; also stones and branches of trees, the fragments of the woods; then flame and fire were used, as soon as they were known; and lastly was discovered the strength of iron and bronze. But the use of bronze was known earlier than that of iron, inasmuch as it is more easy to work and its abundance is greater." Bronze has greatly the antecedence of brass, the former being not less than a score of centuries the more ancient.

Brass is an accidental alloy, formed originally by melting copper in contact with calamine stone (silicate of zinc), the practice, purely empiric, producing what was not known as an alloy, but as a bright copper, valued for its color and other qualities. Certain copper mines were valued as producing this gold-colored copper, but it was found out subsequently that by melting copper with a certain mineral (calamine) the same effect was produced. Aristotle, Strabo, and Albertus Magnus refer to an earth which conferred a yellow color on copper. Sulphate of zinc had a place in the pharmacopœia before its metallic base was known. The metal was discovered by that brilliant absurdity, Paracelsus, in the sixteenth century.

Bronze, on the contrary, has always been recognized as an alloy, being made by the fusing together of copper and tin in suitable proportions. It is found in those countries which possess both of these metals, and also in those ancient lands to which the Phœnicians penetrated. The Malay Islands and Cornwall furnished the tin of antiquity and that of to-day. Australia has also supplied it largely of late. The *kassiteros* (tin) of the Greeks gave its name to Cornwall and Scilly, the kassiterides of Herodotus.[1] It was the *lastera* of the Sanscrit, *kasdir* of the Arabs. The Javanese *tiach*, England *tin*, Swedish *tenn*, and Icelandic *den* mark the limits in either direction of the great traders of the earliest period of history. A bar of tin has been recovered from the Swiss lacustrine piles of Estavayer, molds for hatchets have been found at Morges, and remains of bronze foundries have been uncovered in the Canton of Vaud.[2]

Some of the ancient bronzes of England, Ireland, Scotland, and South America have notable proportions or traces of iron and of lead, and some of them have both of these metals in their composition. In the Roman bronze coins of Pompey, Hadrian, and Probus, zinc, iron, lead, and silver are found. One coin of Tacitus is of copper and iron. These are probably accidental impurities rather than intentional.

The lacustrine researches in the Swiss lakes have given rise to the classification of copper, tin, lead, and zinc as the *principal* ingredients of bronze, and silver, iron, antimony, nickel, and cobalt as *accidental*, and, it may almost be said, unsuspected. The Helvetian bronzes were destitute of lead, and the presence of zinc appears accidental. The use of calamine was common in the Levant, and lead was added to the bronze in notable quantities. In the bronze of the Swiss lakes the copper varied from 67 to 95 per cent., and the tin from 3 to 20 per cent. (Desor). Sir John Lubbock remarks that lead and zinc are not found in the bronzes of the true bronze age.[3]

The iron of early ages, as well as that made by the native workmen of Asia and Africa at the present time, was obtained by a means analogous to that of the Catalan process. The fragments of rich iron ore are distributed through the mass of charcoal in the furnace, and by means of the bellows the fire is urged until the metal runs into a viscid ball, which is hammered to expel the dross, and the steel obtained by the single operation is purified and shaped by successive heatings and hammerings. An excellent quality is obtained, and native weapons were shown at the Centennial from India, Soudan, Angola, Mozambique,

[1] Herodotus, iii, 115.
[2] Elisée Reclus, Smithsonian Report, 1864, p. 357.
[3] Sir John Lubbock's Introduction to Sven Nilson's "Stone Age," page xii.

Zululand, the Gold Coast, Borneo, and the Philippines; also, ancient bronzes from Egypt.

Copper, which may be held to have preceded bronze, was shown in the Indian relics from Wisconsin, and a modern fish-spear of an Alaskan tribe. Copper implements have been found in the lacustrine deposits at Peschiera on Lake Garda.[4]

TYPES OF WEAPONS DESCRIBED.

1. Clubs and throwing weapons.
2. Axes.
3. Knives and swords.

4. Spears.
5. Shields.
6. Bows and arrows.

I.—CLUBS, AND THROWING WEAPONS.

Leaving preambulation, let us begin at the Cape of Good Hope. The *keerie* of the Kafir is his next best weapon after his favorite *assegai*, the native javelin; he does not use the bow and arrow. The *keerie*, called a *knob keerie* by the colonists at the Cape, is a hurling club, or is used in hand to hand encounters, but principally the former. It varies in length from 14 inches to 3 feet, but has been seen as much as six feet long.[5] It is straight and has a knob at the end. It is usually of acacia (*Acacia capensis*), but sometimes of strick wood (*Laurus bullata*). A more costly and highly prized material is rhinoceros horn, of which the *keerie* in the Cape of Good Hope exhibit (shown in the illustration) was made. The *keerie* is habitually carried, and is presented to a friend on meeting him; he touches it, and this is the etiquette of salutation. By a modification of the weapon, giving it a slight bend, it is used in ricochet, rebounding from the ground and striking upward.

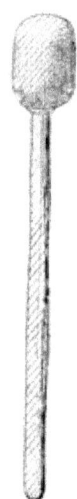

The *knob keerie* of hard black wood is carried by the Bushman also.[6] The *pen bas* of the Bretons has been compared to it.[7]

Fig. 1.—*Kafir Keerie, Cape of Good Hope.*

Coming northward from Zululand we reach the Portuguese Possessions on the east coast of Africa, and find Mozambique weapons; these were shown, together with those from Angola, in the Agricultural Building at the Centennial. Fig. 2 represents two of them; one has a spear-shaped head, and the knob of the other resembles an ear of corn, or the *raceme* of a native plant common in the country. It suggests the idea of maize, but is made by longitudinally grooving, and then notching the protuberant ridges; a not unlikely style of ornamentation for a man to hit upon when amusing himself by carving his weapon. The

---

[4] Marlot, transl. in Smithsonian Report, 1863, p. 373.
[5] Wood's "Natural History of Man," vol. i, p. 108.
[6] Baine's "South Africa," p. 363.
[7] See frontispiece to Trollope's "Walks in Brittany," 2 vols., London, 1840.

clubs of the Dinkas of the Upper Nile[8] are also of hard wood made by ridging and notching so as to leave rows of knobs, like many of the Polynesian weapons. The form resembles the chocolate mullers we used to see, and also suggests the Roman mace *clavnla*.

The club of the Dōrs of the Upper Nile[9] has been compared in shape to the mushroom, having a round disk-shaped head with a sharpened periphery. It is 30 inches in length and made of hard wood. The Djibba club has also a flattened head with a sharp edge, which is guarded by a sheath of hide when not in use. Another club in use in the last-mentioned tribe is champignon-shape, like an unexpanded mushroom. The King of Dahomey[10] is versatile in clubs; one favorite form has a knobbed end and four square knobs at the side; another has a long sharp spike at the end projecting at right angles from the handle.[11]

A variety of sticks and clubs were brought from the different Australian provinces. The peculiar hurling weapons, the *boomerang* and *kangaroo rat*, will be considered presently. Fig. 3 is a Queensland native, armed with his *waddy* and shield. *Waddy* is a native name for a simple club, as shown in Fig. 3, and *b* and *d*, Fig. 4. The knobbed club is known as the *nulla-nulla*, and is shown in Fig. 5, and at *c*, Fig. 4. When the head is flat and sharpened to an edge, the colonists term them *tomahawks*, from their resemblance to the North American Indian weapon. Fig. 4 shows two wooden tomahawks (*a c*) of New South Wales,[12] a *nulla-nulla* (*e*), and two *waddies* (*b d*). The typical Australian *waddy* is 2 feet 8 inches long, weighs 2 pounds, and is made of the heavy and tough mountain tea-tree, box, or red gum wood. It has a pointed end so that its thrust is dangerous.[13]

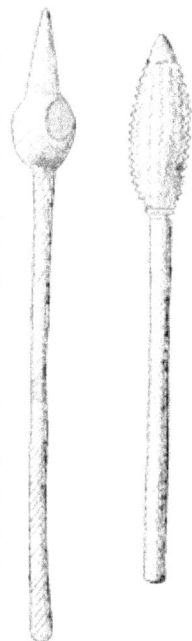

Fig. 3.—*Native Australian with club and shield, Queensland.*

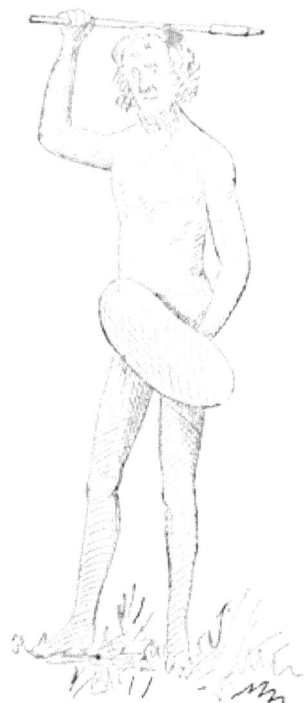

Fig. 2.—*Mozambique Clubs. Portuguese Colonies.*

[8] Wood's "Natural History of Man," vol. i, p. 524.

[9] Wood's "Natural History of Man," i, p. 494.

[10] Duncan's "Western Africa," p. 226.

[11] The knob sticks of the Wanyamnezi are shown in Stanley's "Livingstone," plate opposite page 544.

[12] See the *li-bil*, R. Brough Smith's "Aborigines of Victoria," Fig. 97.

[13] Wood's "Natural History of Man," vol. ii, p. 29.

Some of them have four grooves extending from the point to the hand grasp, so that the wound is something like that made by a bayonet. Fig. 5 shows two *nulla-nullas* or hunting clubs from the southern part of the island, the colony of Victoria. They are two feet long.[14]

The *nulla-nulla* of the Lower Murray River is the *warra-warra* of the Yarra, and is made of a sapling of the mountain tea-tree, the enlargement at the root forming the knob. A pointed *nulla* is made by fashioning one of the projecting roots into a pointed spike, and is called *langeel*.[15] Sharp-edged wooden maces, which may be termed wooden swords, are also made by the Australian natives, some weighing as high as 44 ounces.[16]

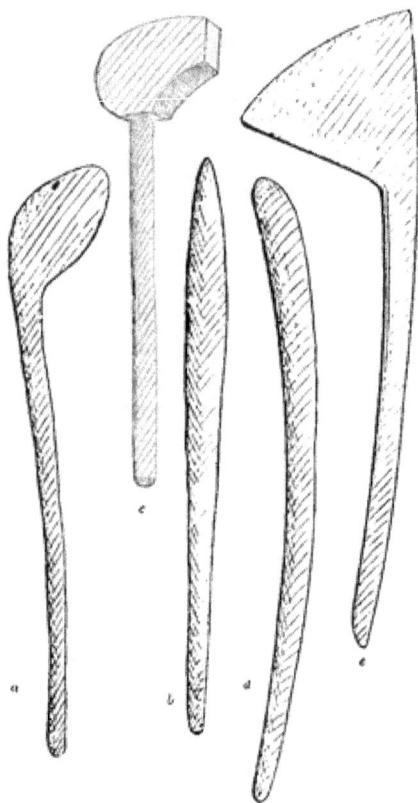

FIG. 4.—*Australian wooden weapons, New South Wales.*

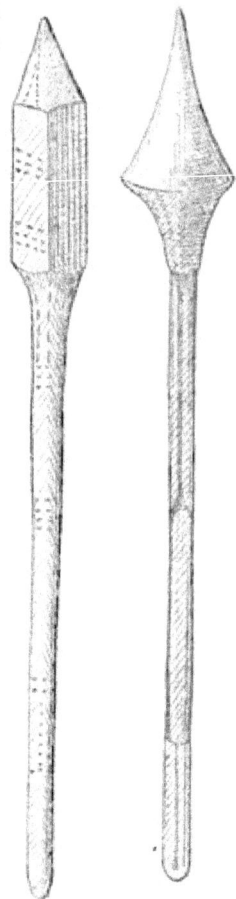

FIG. 5.—*Australian nulla-nullas, Victoria.*

Crossing to New Zealand, we find the Maories to have a much greater variety of material and of shape. The most prized material is the green jade, and it is also wrought with the greatest difficulty. The bone of whale bears a medium character in both respects. Fig. 6 shows two

[14] R. B. Smith's "Aborigines of Victoria," vol. i, 299–300, Figs. 56–59.
[15] *Ibid.*, Fig. 62.
[16] *Ibid.*, Figs. 60, 66, 67; see also Figs. 61, 65.

forms of Maori wooden clubs, known as *pátu;* one has a sharp edge to the axe-like head, and a bunch of feathers intended to shake in the face of an enemy and disturb his aim. The weapon to the right is paddle-shaped, and has two edges; a not uncommon form in Polynesia.

The *merai* or *pátu-pátu* of New Zealand is a two-edged club of a prolonged ovoidal shape. It usually has a hole in the neck for a wrist-cord. Fig. 7 is of green jade, very symmetrical, and beau-

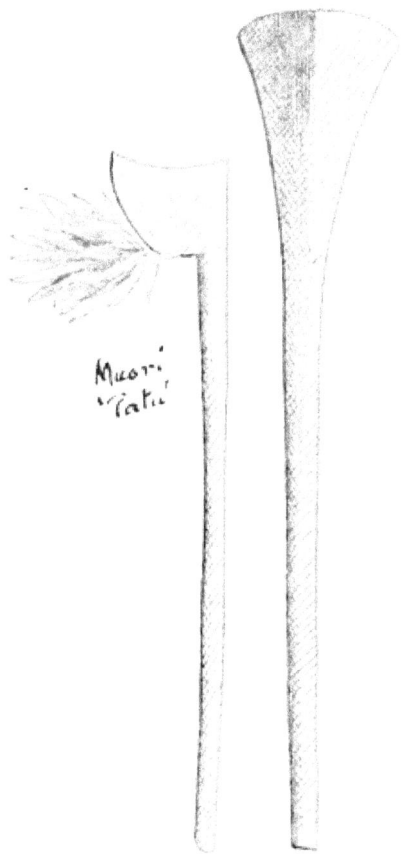

Maori "patu"

FIG. 6.— *Wooden clubs, New Zealand.*

FIG. 7.— *Stone merai, New Zealand.*

FIG. 8.— *Green stone merai, New Zealand.*

tifully polished with a species of corundum found in the island. Fig. 8 is of stone, and is also carefully made and polished. Such weapons become heir-looms in families, and possess names, much as in former times titles were given to swords, as, for instance, *Samsamah,* the cimeter of Haroun al Raschid, and *Excalibar,* the sword of King Arthur. The stone *merai,* Fig. 8, was called *Kororaki.* Fig. 9 is a stone weapon called *Pátu Kohatu;* its wrist-thong occupies a circular depression. Fig. 10 is a carved weapon, the name of which was *Kaikawohi,* or "face-eater." It is made from a bone of a spermaceti whale, and has the reputation of having been handed down in the family for twelve generations. *Merais* of this shape are also made of wood, but are not as much valued as those of harder and more enduring materials.

It had been supposed that the "flattened soda-water-bottle shape," as Tylor has called it, was peculiar to this ingenious cannibal race, the antipodes of the British, but it appears that the Peruvians make a weapon of exactly similar shape; one has been found of dark brown jasper,[17] and another of a greenish amphibolic stone.[18] Another of native copper has been found in Michigan, and was shown at the Centennial. It is 16¼ inches long, 2⅔ inches wide for 11 inches of its length, contracts to 1½ inch, and then enlarges to 2 inches, to assist the hand-grasp. No deduction of importance is to be made from this; the blade is but 1½ inch wider than the handle, and the probability is that the piece of native copper approximated that shape, the work of the owner consisting in flattening, sharpening, and shaping it symmetrically.

Crossing the Southern Ocean we reach the Fiji Islands, lately come into the possession of Great Britain. The Fijian is a Papuan race, and remarkable for constructive ability. The club is his great weapon, and upon it he expends his lavish carving, the implements being of various sizes and patterns, the handiwork being all guided by individual taste.[19] The display at the Centennial was not large, the islands not being specially represented. The classification of their clubs into large, small,

Fig. 9.—*Maori Patu Kohatu. New Zealand.*

Fig. 10.—*Kakati Weapon (bone of whale), New Zealand.*

knobbed, bladed, axe-shaped, straight, or curved gives but a faint idea of the variety. The *dromo* is a spiked mace, and resembles some of the North American Indian clubs. The *dui* is like the double Phrygian axe. The *totokea* is a spiked hammer.[20] The stem of a small tree, with a swelling bole, and the radiating roots trimmed as projecting knobs, is a common style. Another form is made by bending over a young sapling nearly to the ground, so as to bring the tap-root at right angles to the stem. When the tree has sufficiently grown, it is cut and shaped, and the tap-root forms a laterally-projecting knob with a circle of spikes formed of the other roots, shortened and sharpened. Other clubs are like maces; squared and notched; with pyramidal or mushroom tops; ornamented with braided *coir*, with wicker-work, with feathers worked in with *sinnet*, inlaid with shell, bone, hog's tusks, human or whale's teeth.[21]

We miss clubs when we come to lands where the more deadly metal is

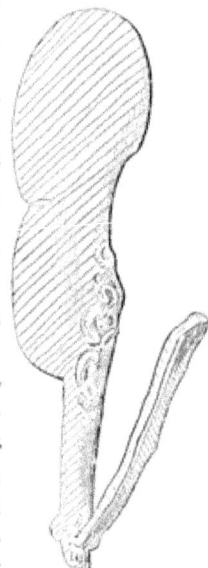

[17] Klemm, C. N., part ii, page 26.
[18] Rivero & Tschudi,' Plates, pl. xxxiii.
[19] Smythe's "Ten Months in Fiji," p. 120.
[20] Williams, "Fiji," pp. 43–4; 589.
[21] Wood, vol. ii, p. 275.

abundant. Java has, however, two clubs deemed worthy of special
names, *Indan* and *Gada*.[22] The
"war-fan" of the Japanese is
perhaps unique, being of large
size and having a sheath of iron
so that it may do duty as a club
on emergency.

Coming to America we find
a greater variety, if possible,
than Fiji furnishes, for those
astute islanders have but a
meager choice of materials—
wood and shell. Fig. 11 is an
Ojibeway war-club from Saga-
mook, on the north shore of
Lake Huron. Fig. 12 shows
two wooden clubs, one armed
with an iron spike; they are
from the Missouri Valley Indians. Spiked weapons have always been
in vogue, and a curious example of one is a
stag's-horn club with the brow
antler left as a spike, found in

Fig. 11.—*Ojibeway wooden club, Can-ada.*

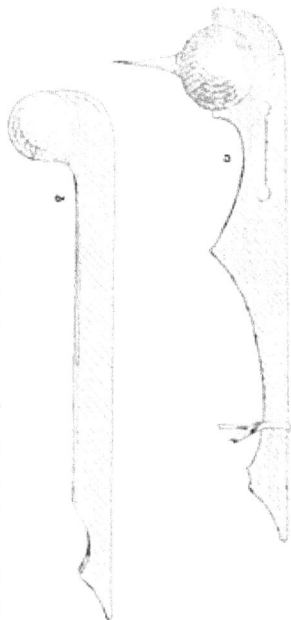

Fig. 12.—*Wooden clubs of Dakotah.—National Museum.*

one of the Swiss Lakes. See memoir by M. E. Desor.[23]
Stag's-horn hammers are also very numerous in the *debris*
of the lake dwellings. A hammer of serpentine with inserted helve and with a hammering face and pointed
peen is mentioned by Nilson.[24] Many other forms are
found among the Indian tribes, but the aim has been to
place together the wooden clubs made in a single piece.
Those in which stones or metal are mounted will be shown
presently. Fig. 13 is a pestle shaped war-
club of the Pai-Utes and Mohaves. They
are termed "face mashers," since they are
carried concealed about the person and
used for striking an enemy in the face.

Figs. 14 and 15 are from the Pacific Coast.
They are elaborately carved war-clubs of
hard wood from the Haidah Indians of
Bella-bella, British Columbia. They are
what we should call "grotesquely carved,"
but the emblems on them are mythological,

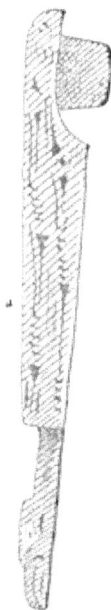

Fig. 14.—*Haidah war-club.—Na-tional Museum.*

and the idea of pleasantry does not, we are
informed, enter into the work. The canoes,
totem-posts, paddles, bowls, and other ob-

Fig. 13.—*Pai-Ute club.—National Mu-seum.*

[22] Sir Stamford Raffles' "Java," 4to ed., i, 296 (Figs. 8, 9).
[23] Translation in Smithsonian Report, 1865, page 357.   [24] Ibid., page 359.

jects fashioned in wood, exhibit the same style of ornamentation, as it must be called.

The Argentine Republic sent a mace, which is shown at Fig. 16. It is of hard wood resembling *lignum vitæ*, and is 18 inches long. It belonged to an Indian of the pampas. A spear eight feet long, of the same kind of wood and tapering to a point, was exhibited with it. The club of the Gran Chaco Indians[25] of the La Plata region is square in section, larger towards each end, and is grasped in the middle. It is called a *macana*, and is used either as a hurling weapon or as a club at close quarters. The clubs of the Guiana Indians are maces of square section, or paddle-shaped with somewhat sharp edges. The handles are embroidered with cotton string, some in a very ornamental manner. The Uaupé Indians of the Amazon[26] also use carved wooden clubs.

We come now to a class of clubs in which a stone is mounted upon a withe or other kind of handle to form a maul or hammer. We do not in the present article consider those which have sharp edges, and are designed to form axes and adzes. They will be grouped separately. Fig. 17 is about as primitive an affair as can well be devised.

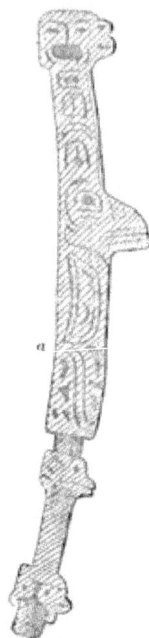

Fig. 15.—*Haidah carved war-club.—National Museum.*

Fig. 16.—*Mace from Paraguay, Argentine Confederation.*

It is a shell-headed club from a shell-heap on Saint John's River, Florida. The head is a *Pyrula*, and the specimen is peculiar in this, that though ancient it still has the remains of the original handle.

In connection with this method of mounting, by a perforated head through which the helve is thrust, mention may be made of hammer stones, sometimes known as helved wedges, similarly handled, and which have been hurling axes. They are more frequent in Europe than in America. Some

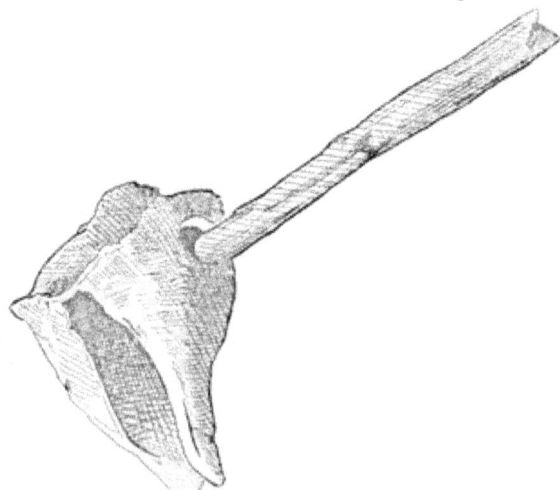

Fig. 17.—*Shell-headed club from a Florida shell-heap.—National Museum.*

of these have their edges in line with the handle and some across it, as axes and adzes respectively.   See Sven Nilson's " Stone Age,"[27] edited by Sir John Lubbock.   A re-markable four-pronged stone battle-axe is shown in the mu-seum of Lund, Sweden, hav-ing a diameter of 8 inches, and perforated for a handle.[28]

Fig. 18 is a stone maul lashed with raw-hide thongs to a T-shaped handle which has been formed from a forked branch. It is from the Haidah Indians. Bella-bella, British Columbia. Fig. 19 is a large stone maul lashed to a short handle formed of a forked limb. It is from Sitka, Alaska. Fig. 20 is from New Zealand. It shows that a similar mode of mounting is practiced by the Maories, the bowlder being secured in the crotch by means of thongs. The pursuit of similar examples leads us a devious dance.

FIG. 18.—Stone maul, from British Columbia.—National Museum.

FIG. 19.—Stone maul of Alaska.—National Museum.

We find that the Gran Chaco Indians, of South America, have a peculiar method of embedding a cylindrical stone in a club so that it may project

FIG. 20.—Maori stone club, New Zealand.

like an axe blade. A hole is bored into a sapling of suitable size and the stone driven in. As the tree grows, the wood advances upon the stone and grips it firmly. The sapling is then cut and shaped.

FIG. 21.—Stone maul of Arickarees.

Fig. 21 is a stone maul of the Arickaree Indians of the Upper Missouri River.[29] It is a reddish, granite pebble of three and a half pounds

[27] Page 72, and plate ix, Figs. 1-3, 1-4; pp. 73, 74; and plate viii, Figs. 180, 181.
[28] Ibid., page 75, and pl. ix, Fig. 159.
[29] See "Twenty-first Report of N. Y. State Cabinet," pp. 31-36, pls. i, ii, iii.

weight. The withe is bent around it, occupying a circumferential depression, which is interrupted opposite the handle. The same kind of hammer was used by the native workmen formerly in the Lake Supe-

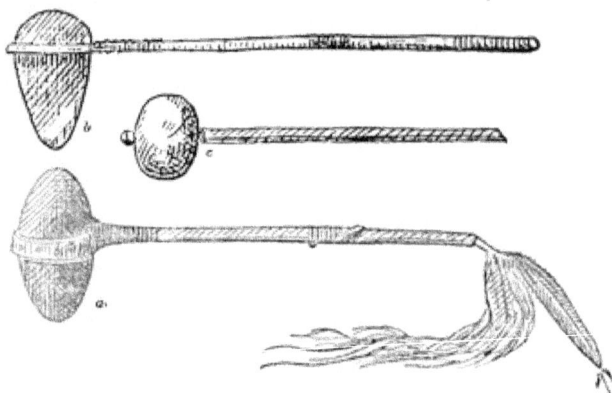

FIG. 22.—Stone mauls of Missouri Valley Indians.—National Museum.

rior copper mines. It is used by the Missouri Indians in driving stakes and tent-pegs.

Fig. 22 shows two stone implements of the Sioux, the hereditary enemies of the tribe last mentioned. The upper one is a rude grooved axe mounted in a hickory sapling, the two ends of which are brought together with raw-hide thongs to form the handle. The lower figure is a war-club with an egg-shaped limestone head and a handle of ash; the end of the latter is ornamented with the tuft from the tail of a buffalo. Between the two figures is a representation of the Roman sacrificial *mallens*, which, even in the time of the emperors, was employed in slaughtering the victims. It seems to have come down from times then ancient, the order of procedure admitting of no innovation, just as the knives of flint were used in ancient Egypt and among the Hebrews in performing ceremonial observances and sacrifices. Dr. Schliemann found hundreds of rude stone hammers in the hill of Hissarlik.

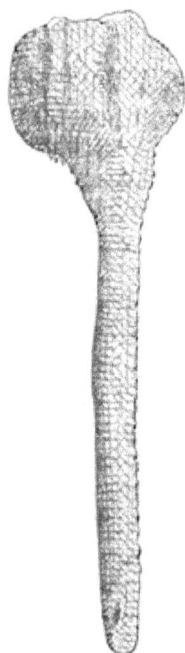

Another mode of mounting a large pebble or wedge-shaped stone is by means of a raw-hide covering to the stone and withe.

FIG. 23.—Arickaree stone maul.

FIG. 24.—War-club of Apaches. Arizona.—National Museum.

Fig. 23 shows an Arickaree weapon made in this manner: The granite pebble weighing 22 ounces is grooved circumferentially and a withe bent around it and secured by raw-hide thongs next to the stone. Over the whole of the stone and handle, except the hammer face, a single piece of wet buffalo hide is stretched and sewed with sinew. When the hide shrinks in drying the whole forms a very firm job. The use of a similar tool in driving stakes and tent-pins has been mentioned, but there are many other purposes about an Indian camp, such as breaking bones and pounding pemmican, for which it is well adapted, not to mention the warlike uses.

The *poggamoggon* of the Shoshones is a slungshot.

Fig. 24 shows yet another mode of mounting the stone. The pebble and the withe are covered with the tail skin of a buffalo, the tuft of hair remaining. It resembles the slungshot used nearer home, or the stone in a stocking foot, said to be a favorite with the gentler sex in some places.

Hammer-axes of stone and horn, bored for the helve, are to be found in many museums. See Nilson.[30]

We will now examine the throwing weapons; premising that neither law nor custom prevents the hurling of some already described. The Fijian among the abundance of his clubs has one specially for throwing; it is knobbed at the end like the Kafir *keerie* and is worn in the girdle, sometimes in pairs like pistols. Fig. 25 is the throwing-stick of Uganda

FIG. 25.—*Throwing-stick of Uganda, Africa.—Egyptian Exhibit.*

brought by Capt. Long (Bey) from his expedition south of Khartoom. It is three feet long, has a spear-shaped head, and is hurled with a whirling motion somewhat in the manner of the Australian *boomerang*, but without the peculiar erratic flight of the latter.

The curved throwing-stick was also noticed by Sir Samuel Baker in Abyssinia, and is common among the negroes as far west as Lake Tsad. The *Es-sellem* of the desert[31] is like the curved sticks of the ancient Egyptians[32] and closely resembles the middle stick in Fig. 28.

The *trumbash* or throwing-stick of the Niam-niams of the Upper Nile[33] is a flat projectile used for killing birds or hares, and is carried inside the shield. The war weapon when made of iron is called *kulbeda*, and has three projecting limbs with pointed prongs and sharp edges, the longer blade at right angles to the grip, which is guarded by the shortest prong of the three. This wicked weapon is spun about its axis and

[30] "Stone Age" Pl. viii, Figs. 162–179.
[31] Smith's "Aborigines of Victoria," Discussion on, pp. 321 et seq., vol. i.
[32] Ibid (note passim), i, 299.
[33] Schweinfurth.

has a movement of translation in a horizontal plane. It is also a hack-
ing hand-to-hand weapon. Somewhat similar weapons with two blades
are found in upper Sennaar and Central Soudan, and are used by the
Fans. The *keerie* or knobbed throwing-stick of the Kafirs has been
already described. The *lissan* is the curved throwing-stick of another

FIG. 26.—*Niam-niam hurling-weapons (trumbash).*

African tribe; the iron *hungamunga*[34] of the Tibbus and of Darfur is also
a hurling weapon. [35]

It would be singular, indeed, if a cudgel for throwing at game were
found in but one part of the world, and at but one period; but the discovery of the Australian *boomerang*, the most curious of its class, has
directed attention to what might otherwise have been passed over as
unimportant. The Egyptian and Assyrian monuments have been con-
sulted, and in each case the curved stick has been noticed in the hands
of bird-catchers or hunters. An ancient throwing-stick about eighteen
inches long is in the Abbott Egyptian collection of the New York Historical Society. A short, crooked stick (*pedum*) was used by the Romans
to throw at hares, and centaurs are represented with a short *pedum*
(λαγωβόλον) in the other.

In coming to Australia we reach a people living in an almost primitive condition, so low, ill-formed, and ignorant that their name has become a synonym for imbecility. Here, however, the throwing-stick has
attained its highest development. The maximum of improvement has

---

[34] Illustrated in the discussion on the boomerang. Smith, "Abor. Victoria," 321 *et
seq.*
[35] Tyler's "Early History of Mankind," 175-6. See also paper by Ferguson in Trans.
R. I. A. Dublin, 1843, vol. xix. Paper by W. Cooke Taylor. The Nat. Hist. Soc.
London, 1840, vol. i, page 205; Eyre, vol. ii, p. 305; Klemm, C. G. vol. i, p. 316, plate vii.

not, however, been reached by the natives of all parts of this island, which is almost as large as the United States and Territories. The *boomerang* (Fig. 27), used with such singular dexterity by the "black

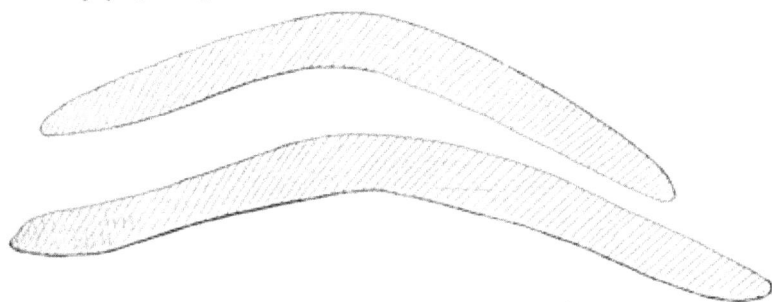

FIG. 27.—*Boomerangs of New South Wales.*

fellows" of New South Wales, is almost unknown to those of the colony of South Australia, which, by the bye, is not the most southerly portion of the island, that position being occupied by the thriving colony of Victoria. The boomerang is, however, used in Western Australia, where it is called a *ky-lie*. This is a true return-boomerang.[36] Even in the districts where the *boomerang* is used there are all grades of throwing-sticks, three of which of different forms were in the New South Wales exhibit, and are shown in Fig. 28. The upper one is carved with raised serpentine figures, the stick being painted red in the intervals. With these weapons the natives give a direct blow, a whirling blow, or a ricochet upward-rebounding blow.

The *boomerang* is made of the wood of the blue gum (*Eucalyptus glob-*

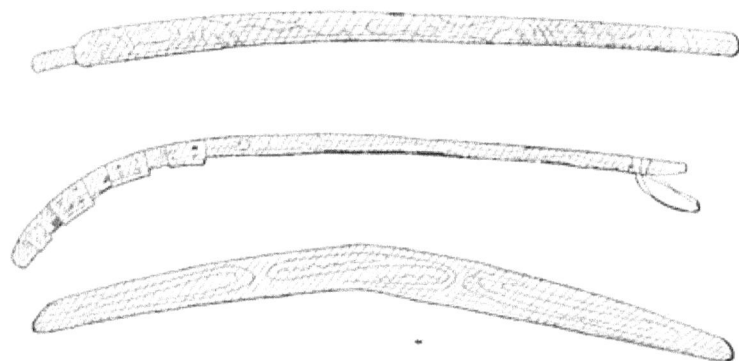

FIG. 28.—*Australian throwing-sticks, Victoria.*

ulus), or sometimes from the iron-bark of the she-oak, and is of flatted curved shape, convex on the upper surface and flat below, always thickest in the middle, from which it is scraped away towards both edges, which are tolerably sharp, especially the outer one. *Boomerangs* vary much in shape, but do not depart from the characteristics mentioned. They differ in their curves, lengths, widths, taper, and weight.

---

[36] Aborigines of Victoria, vol. i, 336, Fig. 140.

A good specimen may be 33 inches from tip to tip measured along the curve, 2 inches wide, and weigh 12 ounces. There are several ways of throwing the boomerang so as to make it execute its peculiar evolutions. In throwing it, the native grasps it by the handle end, which has some notches upon it, and holds the flat side downward; then balancing it a moment in his hand, and making a few quick steps forward, he launches it with a sharp fling, bringing his hand back so as to make it revolve in the plane of its curve with great rapidity. The peculiarity of the boomerang is in what may be considered its erratic flight. Thrown so as to strike the ground 40 yards in advance of the thrower, it rebounds, describes a high circular backward course, and falls behind the thrower. Thrown high in the air it mounts to a great height, circles backward until its force is expended, and then drops dead at a point behind the thrower. It is also thrown, so as at a given distance to make its rebound in other than an upward circular direction, and curve its flight around an object so as to strike something behind the latter. This is merely an effort of skill. The *boomerang* is thrown against the wind; and, though it is easy enough to hurl it, it is very difficult to make it perform at command all the peculiar evolutions which distinguish it. It is roughly made, so far as mere finish is concerned; but the work upon it in adjusting the curves is most scrupulously and patiently performed by the natives, some of whom never acquire proficiency, while others become celebrated for their skill in the manufacture of the weapon. Like all instruments which have attained something like perfection, the difference between the best and poorest is greater than in the case of some other tools where a more general level of excellence is preserved.

The subject of the *boomerang* has been learnedly and carefully considered in R. Brough Smith's "Aborigines of Victoria."[37] The discussion has elicited the fact that some throwing-sticks move with a spinning or whirling motion, and even pursue a curved path, as a billiard or baseball player can curve the trajectory by imparting rotation to the ball. None of the implements, however, described by Col. Lane Fox (British Association, 1872), or referred to in Mr. Ferguson's learned paper before the Royal Irish Academy in 1838, are fairly comparable to the Australian weapon. It must also be remarked that the distinction between the play weapon and the war weapon is clearly drawn in the mind of the native, though the back-return boomerang cannot always be distinguished from the war boomerang by a novice. The *barageet* of the Yarra,[38] for instance, is a war weapon, and not a come-back; nor is it so much curved as the regular boomerang, *wonguim*.[39] A group of the various kinds is shown in Mr. Smith's work, previously referred to.[40]

From the straight round stick, knobbed stick, flat stick, curved stick, edged curved stick (a wooden sword), through every degree of curvature up to the perfect boomerang, the series of Australian hurling weapons occupies the whole ground. The most curiously-curved weapon,

[37] Vol. i, p. 321, et seq.   [38] Ibid., Fig. 96.   [39] Ibid., Fig. 95.   [40] Ibid., i, 315, Fig. 99.

which should not be omitted, is the *quirriang-an-wun*, impossible to explain without an illustration, and not shown in Philadelphia. It is a thin flake of wood, curiously twisted and curved.[41]

Fig. 29 shows, for purposes of comparison, an Australian *boomerang* (*a*) from Murray River, and a curved throwing-stick (*b*) used by the Moqui and Shimmo Indians in killing rabbits. These throwing-sticks, though

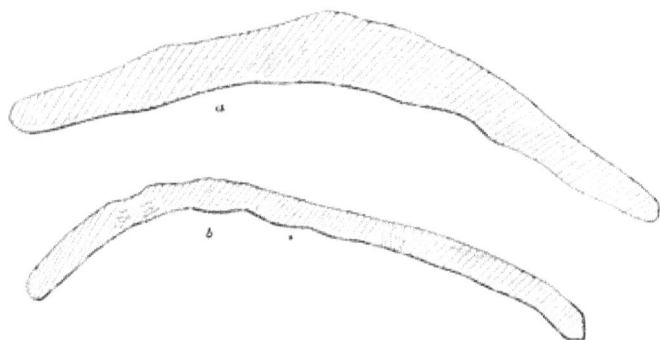

Fig. 29.—*Boomerang and Moqui throwing-stick.*

curved so as to resemble in one important respect the Australian weapon, cannot, like it, be made to describe the peculiar divergent curved course through the air. These sticks were formerly used by many of the Southern California tribes.

The *kangaroo rat* (*weet-weet*),[42] Fig. 30, of the Australians has been

Fig. 30.—*Kangaroo rat, South Australia.*

sometimes spoken of as rather a toy than a weapon, but it is a dangerous missile. Its head is usually a piece of hard wood, of a conoidal or double conical shape, and its tail is a flexible handle a yard long. By this handle it is thrown; the native takes the *rat* by the *tail* and swings it back and forth several times, bending it almost double. Suddenly letting it fly by an underhand jerk, it glides hissing through the air, striking and rebounding like a flat stone skimming the surface of the water—the familiar "ducks and drakes" of our childhood. It does not rise more than nine feet above the surface of the ground, and the distance it reaches depends upon the force of the projection and also upon the angle at which it first strikes the surface of the earth. If the trajectory be too high, it makes a number of high leaps and soon tires; if too low, the force is soon expended in friction on the ground. The body with a trailing tail making flying leaps has much the appearance of a small

---

[41] *Ibid.*, i, 315, Fig. 315.
[42] Wood, ii, p. 41.

kangaroo, and is well named the *kangaroo rat.* The example illustrated is of wild buffalo horn, heated and pressed to shape.

The kangaroo rat described by R. Brough Smith is about 26 inches long, the tail being 21 inches and the head 4.5 inches.[43]

Something like the kangaroo rat of the Australians is a missile employed in a game of the Fijians.[44] A reed four feet in length terminates in an ovoid piece of hard and heavy wood six inches long. It is held between the thumb and finger and thrown by an underhand jerk, so as to skim horizontally over the ground. A long smooth stretch of turf is kept in good order in the villages for this purpose. This suggests the pitching of quoits and horseshoes, curling stones, hockey, polo, and other ball games, which we merely suggest as we pass, supposing them not to be distinctly savage, though some of them are athletic survivals of ancient barbaric exercises.

The *chakra*[45] or "quoit weapon" of the Sikhs is savage enough to be worth a mention. It is an annular disk of thin steel with a sharp edge all round. It is whirled upon the fore-finger and then thrown, spinning as it flies, and is a formidable weapon when aimed at the face of an enemy, several being hurled in rapid succession and with great force. They can also give it a ricochet flight.

A similar weapon has been brought from Guatemala by M. Boursier, the French Consul. It is disk-shaped, very sharp on the edges, and about 6 inches in diameter. Hurling-disks have been found also in Brittany and Central France.

The Peruvian hurling-disk is of diorite with a central opening 1 inch in diameter and 10 circumferential teeth 2 inches long. It is thrown by aid of a thong like the bolus. The Mexicans have a similar weapon[46] and the Australians a crude affair of the same general idea.

From this cutting disk whirled by the finger we reach by a single step the simple pebble which is hurled by hand. We began with a stick, and after considering the club simple and compound, and the various forms of throwing clubs, have come to simple missiles—the pebble or small bowlder. Some tribes, however, are not content with the stones of the brook, but shape the projectile; the Tahitians,[47] for instance, make oval balls of stalagmite, which they hurl by hand with force and accuracy, not using a sling. The Fuegians, although very skillful with the sling, are adepts at hurling stones by hand.

Incendiary balls were used by the Nervii, who fired the camp of Cæsar, and the balls of charcoal kneaded with clay, and found in the lacustrine village remains in Switzerland, are believed to have been for the same purpose. The arrow with a lighted tow torch is commonly noticed among the ancients, and is found in all parts of the world where the bow and arrow survive.

---

[43] Aborigines of Australia, i, Fig. 170, p. 352.   [44] Wood, ii, p. 283.
[45] Wood, i.   [46] Louvre collection.   [47] Wood, ii.

The subject here naturally diverges and takes two separate paths. The projectile is loose and is hurled by a stick or a sling; or it is attached to a string which flies with it. We shall consider these separately and in the order stated.

The sling is an unimpressive object when hung up among a thousand other things in a collection, and how many were overlooked by the writer at the Centennial it is not possible to say. The example, Fig. 31, was in the National Museum exhibit in the Government Building, having been obtained from the Navajoes of New Mexico. Slings are rarely used among this people at present, except by boys. They are, however, mentioned in the old account of the "Journey to the Seven Cities of Cibola." There is no doubt about the antiquity of the device. It is mentioned frequently in the Hebrew writings, and is shown on the Egyptian [48] and Assyrian monuments. [49] The Roman sling was named from its *funda* or purse which contained the projectile. Besides its ordinary use for hurling stones, leaden balls (*glandes*) were used; these were ellipsoidal plummets, often with inscriptions upon them, as " FIR," for *firmiter*, " throw steadily "; Grecian bullets also, marked with the figure of a thunderbolt, or the inscription δέξαι, " take this," have been found. Schliemann [50] recovered from the excavations at Hissarlik sling-bullets of loadstone, copper, alabaster, and diorite. The *fustibolus* was a four-foot pole, which had a sling attached in the center, enabling both hands to be used in throwing.

Fig. 31.—Navajo sling.—National Museum.

The sling is not so universal a weapon that a statement of the countries where it is used becomes a mere geographical recitation. The Javan sling [51] (*bandring*) is noticed by Sir Stamford Raffles. The Fijians, as already stated, excel in its use. The sling of the Sandwich Islanders [52] is a double thong with a stone receptacle of plaited sinnet. The stones are egg-shaped and ground for the purpose. Another form of Hawaiian sling has an oval stone with a circumferential groove, and is hurled by a cord passed around it and secured by a sailor's half-hitch so as to be released when the thong is jerked back to discharge the stone. A similar mode of hurling the spear is found in South America. The Marquesas Islanders [53] use slings of plaited grass, as much as five feet in length, and hurl stones of considerable size. The natives of New Caledonia [54] have a sling (*wendat*) which is a double thong with a purse in the middle made of two parallel cords. The stones are a hard kind of steatite ground to an oval shape and polished. They are carried in a net at the right side and are discharged after a half whirl of the sling. Some of

[48] Kitto, i, 370.
[49] Layard's Nineveh, Pls. vi, vii, ii, 263. Xenophon's Anabasis, *lib.* iii, c. 3.
[50] Schliemann's " Troy and its Remains," 104. Nos. 66-7-8.
[51] " Java," 4to, Pl. iv, opp. p. 296, vol. i; Fig. 22.
[52] Wood, ii, p. 434.   [53] *Ibid.*, ii, p. 390.   [54] *Ibid.*, ii, p. 205.

the New Caledonian sling-stones are shaped like two spherical segments, joined at their bases, giving a sharp circumferential ridge. The same form is found in New Zealand and in the stone age missiles of Sweden.

Wooden slings and ribbon slings were used by the ancient inhabitants of Sweden, and slings of bast are in the museums of Lund and Stockholm.[55] Slings of plaited flax are among the lacustrine remains of Neufchâtel.[56]

The Solomon Islanders also use slings. The Fuegians[57] excel in the use of the sling, as well as of the bow and arrow and spear. The sling has a pocket of seal or guanaco skin and two thongs three feet in length of twisted sinews. The natives throw with great force and accuracy.

Pliny ascribes the invention of the sling to the Phœnicians. He always had a guess to make; sometimes a very wild one. The Balearic Islanders[58] were celebrated for their expertness in its use. The slingers of the Greek and Roman armies were considered an inferior class of warriors, the sling being but an auxiliary weapon.

Another mode of slinging is by means of a stick thrust through a perforated stone and whirled so as to discharge the missile when it has attained a maximum centrifugal motion.

Fig. 32 shows two throwing-stones from Peru, adapted to be slung by a stick which is thrust into the hole. The Peruvians were very expert in the use of the sling.[58] Whorls of star shape were found in great quantities by Schliemann in the excavations at Hissarlik.[59] Although they may be considered spindle

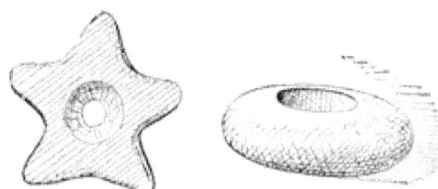

FIG. 32.—Throwing-stones, Peru.

whorls, it is altogether probable, so great was their number, that they were ammunition. Disk-shaped and cylindrical throwing-stones perforated for the stick are found among the remains of the Lake Dwellers.[60] The Fijians have a rough game of jerking stones at each other with elastic bamboo.[61]

Numerous stones fashioned into shapes, and many of them with circumferential grooves, are to be found in European and American collections, labelled *plummets* (net-sinkers), *sling-stones*, &c., according to the fancy or opinion of the discoverer or owner. The same may be said of American perforated stones which may be plummets or gorgets. There is a tendency to give a warlike signification to such finds recovered in the soil, in mounds or in graves. The civil uses of these objects were probably much more frequent than the warlike; as the search for food is a

[55] Sven Nilson "On the Stone Age."   Ed. by Sir John Lubbock, pl. v, pp. 49, 53.
[56] Morlot in Smithsonian Report, 1863, p. 377.   [57] Wood, ii, p. 517.
[58] Cæsar's Comm., ii, 1.   [58] Prescott's "Conquest of Peru," i, 72.
[59] "Troy and its Remains," No. 444, Pl. xl.
[60] "Culturgeschichte." Taf. 2, Figs. 60–63.   [61] Wood, ii.

more constant occupation than war.   (Cf. Sven Nilson, edited by Sir John Lubbock, London, 1868.)[62]

We now pursue the other branch of the section, in which the ball remains attached to the cord by means of which it is projected. The simplest form of this is the single stone or metallic ball sewed up in rawhide and attached to the end of a thong a yard long. This, the *bolas perdida* of the Spaniards, is whirled rapidly around the head and then launched at the enemy or the game. A similar ball at the end of a shorter thong is used as a sling-shot.

The *bolas*[63] of South America consists of two or three balls at the ends of as many raw-hide thongs, about nine feet long, which are tied together. The *bolas* is swung around the head of the rider, the junction of the thongs being in his hand and the balls flying in a cluster. As soon as they are launched at the game, the balls fly apart by their centrifugal force, and, still flying round, have a movement of translation in the direction of their projection. As soon as a thong strikes the object, the balls coil around it in contrary directions, binding and entangling it according to the intention of the thrower. This is not too much to say, for the Patagonian will bind the rider to the horse, or tie the legs of an animal together or to the body at will. Stones of ovoid form made of trachytic tufa and perforated for raw-hide straps are used by the California Indians.

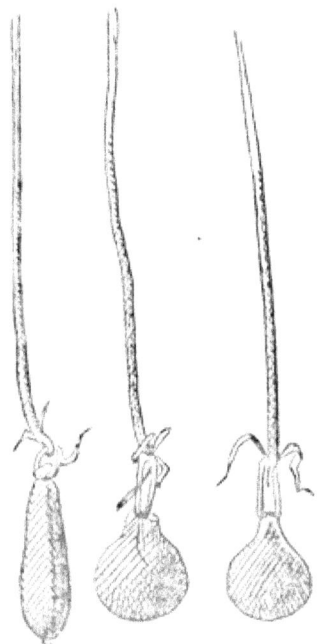

Fig. 33.—*Bolas of Paraguay, Argentine Confederation.*

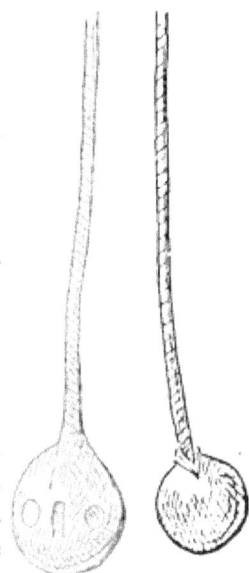

Fig. 34.—*Bolas of Argentine Republic.*

Figs. 33 and 34 show the *bolas* exhibited at the Centennial by the Argentine Republic. They consist of stones or balls of clay in raw-hide pockets at the ends of twisted thongs of raw-hide. The specimens differ much in weight, from one-quarter of a pound to one and a half pounds, and in size from one and a quarter inches to three inches in diameter. They are sewed up in their envelopes, and in one case openings are made to expose the bright red color of a peculiar stone of the country. It is the duty of

[62] Sven Nilson, Pl. ix, Fig. 216; Pl. ii, Fig. 31-35.   [63] Page's "La Plata," 112.

the women to cut and grind these stones, but in some cases iron or even copper balls are used, the metal being preferred when attainable on account of its being smaller for a given weight. There is some variation in the arrangement also : (*somai*) two *bolas* at the end of 9-feet thongs; (*achico*) three *bolas*, one on a rather longer thong; or one of the thongs has attached to its mid-length a pair of balls on the end of three-foot thongs. The range of the *bolas* is from 30 to 40 yards. The natives, when in danger, wear several cuirasses of stiff raw-hide as a guard against them, the armor being put on like a poncho—over the head, which is thrust through a slit in the hide. The helmet is of double bull-hide. The *bolas* is used throughout the Argentine Republic, by the Gran Chaco Indians of La Plata, the Araucanians (called by them *laqui*), and the Patagonians; being, in a large portion of the territory mentioned, the principal means of capturing wild animals. The guanaco, a species of llama about the size of a deer, is the main dependence for food and clothing of the Patagonians.[64]   See Muster's account of the Tehuelche Indians.[65]

Passing at one bound to the other extremity of the American Continent, we find the Eskimo[66] in possession of the same weapon, but on a smaller scale, as befits the game it is intended to capture. It consists of eight or nine strings, about thirty inches long, and fastened together, their free ends being attached to little weights like plumb-bobs, made of bone, walrus-tooth, or stone. The cords are of twisted sinews or intestines. The balls are whirled around the head two or three times and then sent flying through the air like a large cobweb, lapping with surprising quickness around any object which may be struck by the cords. It is used principally in catching birds.

The lasso was shown in the exhibit of the Argentine Confederation, in the main building. It is a rope 40 feet long, made of raw-hide strips plaited into a round rope, excepting a few feet at the noose end, which is plaited square and is fastened around an iron ring, through which the lasso passes to form the noose. The Araucanians use a lasso of silk-grass fiber from the leaves of an agave. It has no ring for the noose, but a loop of the agave fiber covered with leather. In using the lasso, the ring is taken in the left hand and a noose six feet in length is made; the right hand then grasping the cord and the ring, the rider takes another six feet in his hand and whirls the noose around his head until it becomes circular, when he hurls it at the object, throwing after it the remainder of the rope, which hangs in coils on his left arm. As it passes through the air the noose becomes smaller, so that the diameter of the noose is graduated to the size of the object it is intended to capture. It is not a little singular that this form of lasso, a noose running in a metallic ring, was a weapon in the armies of the former Singhalese monarch.[67]

---

[64] Wood, ii., p. 532.   [65] "At Home with the Patagonians," p. 166.
[66] Wood, ii., p. 711.   [67] Tennent's "Ceylon," i, 499.

A strangling noose, a few feet long, with a bone or wooden pointed stick at one end and a worked eye at the other, is used by the Australian to garrote a sleeping enemy. Passing the noose over the head and thrusting the skewer through the loop, he throttles his victim, who is powerless to make a noise, and, throwing him over his shoulder, carries him from the camp.[69]

II.—AXES.

If the name of a tool is to be determined by its shape and mode of usage, the first axe was of wood. The Australian department showed several bludgeons, the enlarged flattened ends of which had sharp edges. Being of blue gum (*Eucalyptus globulus*), a hard heavy wood, they are efficient weapons in war or in hunting, though not suitable for felling timber. They are shown at *a b*, in Fig. 35; *c d* are from New Zealand, and *e* is from the Haidah Indians of Bella-Bella, British Columbia.

The transition from one material to another may be traced in many countries in yet-existing tools; the change is one of the most interesting problems of the archaist and ethnologist, and it is recognized in a Chinese tradition: " Fuhi made weapons; these were of wood; those of Shinnung were of stone; then Chi-yu made metallic ones."

After the club or sling-stone, in which a bowlder is mounted on a withe, or bound to a stick, or slung at the end of a raw-hide thong, comes an attempt to give a cutting edge to the tool. It need not be merely assumed, as it is capable of demonstration, that the mounting of unwrought spalls of stone preceded the fashioning of stone axes. The

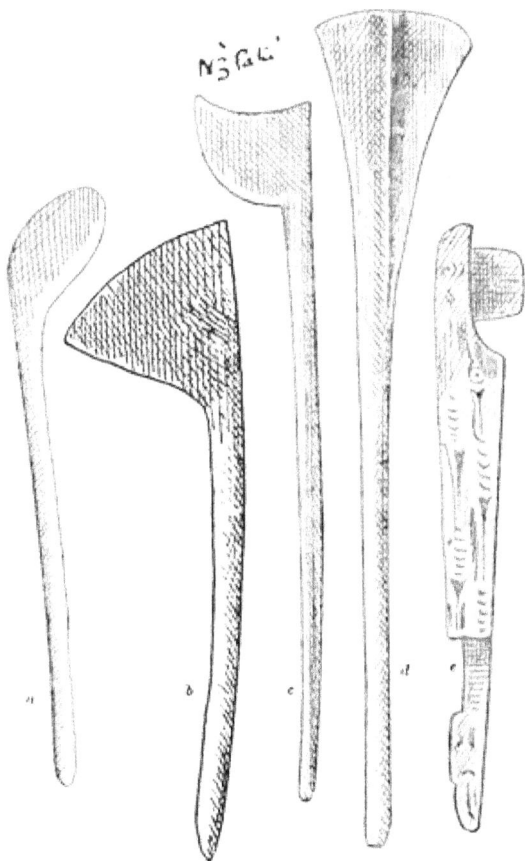

FIG. 35.—*Wooden axes, from Australia, New Zealand, and British Columbia.*

[69] Smith's " Aborigines of Victoria," i, 351, Fig. 169.

New South Wales exhibit showed a collection of spalls of greenstone and sandstone obtained by the natives by merely dashing bowlders together and picking up the pieces which most nearly approximated the desired form. Those shown in the collection were of sandstone, con-

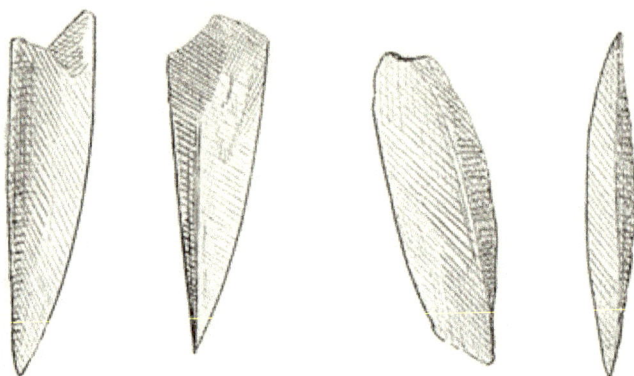

FIG. 36.—*Stone spalls for axes, Clarence River, New South Wales.*

glomerate, slate, basalt, and trachyte. Such axes, when helved, are used by the natives in ascending and for felling trees, cutting firewood, in war and the chase, and for cutting themselves to embellish their bodies with cicatrized wounds.

In many countries are to be found famous localities yielding stones for axes. In Nan-hin-fu, in the province of Kwantong, in Southern China,[69] they find in the mountains a heavy stone, which furnishes materials for cutting-tools for the region around. Obsidian is used in Mexico, Khamschatka,[70] and elsewhere.

The stone axes and adzes of the Philadelphia Exhibition may be considered together. The difference in the tools is in the relation of the cutting edge to the handle. In the axe the line of the edge is in the plane of the handle. In the adze the edge is across the plane of its sweep. The examples afforded us may be classed in two divisions: first, stone and shell; second, metal. The subdivision which will be most useful will be as to the four methods of mounting the axe-head in or on the handle; and we have instances of each in the stone axes, and of three out of the four in the metallic axes, and this without going outside of the crude implements shown in Philadelphia.

The four modes of mounting or helving an axe are:

1. By winding a withe around it.
2. By lashing it to a seat on the handle.
3. By passing the tang through a hole in the handle.
4. By passing the helve through a hole in the head.

[69] Grosier, "*De la Chine*," Paris, 1818, i, 191.
[70] Erman, "*Reise*," iii, 453.

Before adducing examples of each of these methods, we may simply notice the stone hatchet from New Zealand, which is used independently of a handle, and is a hand-to-hand weapon, like some of the *meraisor pátu-pátus*, shown in a previous ar-

Fig. 37.—*Maori stone hatchet, New Zealand.*

ticle, and considered characteristic of the Maori race.

While some of the methods of securing the axe-head to the helve are considered indicative of certain tribes and peoples, it cannot be said that any peculiar mode is found at a certain place or in such a tribe and nowhere else. In fact, it may be stated that among the various tribes of North American Indians all the modes cited may be found, and specimens from the lacustrine dwellings, to be seen in the museums of Europe and America, show that all the modes stated were in use among the early inhabitants of Europe.

Fig. 38 shows three native stone axes: *a* from Victoria, *b* from South Australia, and *c* from the Sioux country of the Missouri Valley. They agree in the mode of fastening the head to the handle, a withe being bent around a depression in the stone and secured by lashings; these will depend upon the material at hand. In the case of the stone axe (*mogo*) *a*, from Victoria, the head is a chipped greenstone 2 by 4 inches, and is mounted in a withe with moss and "black-boy gum." The weapon (*a*) is far in advance of the art of the present natives, who use the rudest stone axes, mere spalls, as just described, and

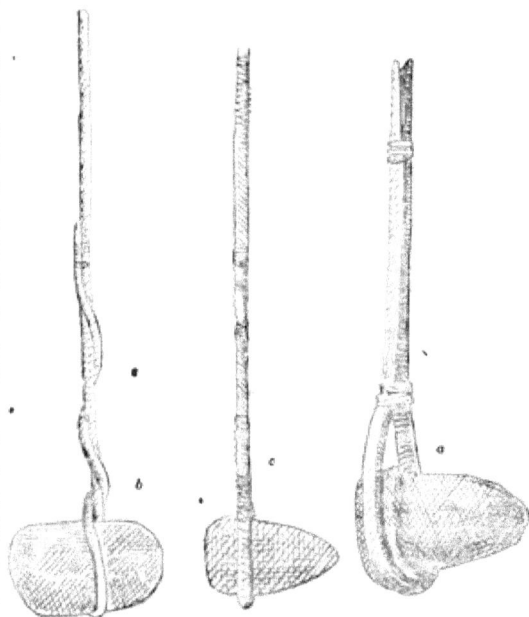

Fig. 38.—*Stone axes of Australia and America.*

shown in Fig. 36. The natives say that this *mogo* was made by a people who preceded them and of whom they have no knowledge. It need not on that account be necessarily very old, but it seems that it was somewhat of a local curiosity to the particular tribe in which it was found.

The *kad jo, mo-go,* and other stone tomahawks of Australia are well delineated and described in a careful treatise just published by R.

Brough Smith.[71] They are of granite, quartz, &c., one edge chipped sharp, a poll left relatively flat; all adapted to be handled with withes, unground, and secured by gum.

In New South Wales the natives take for the handle the flowering stem of the *waratah* or native tulip, or the vine of *pepperoma*, or they carefully split the small water gum of the streams, and, by the action of fire, make the piece pliant and wrap it like a withe around the stone axe-head. They next take the resinous and brittle gum of the grass-tree (*Xanthorhœa*), which they knead and toughen by the fire process. With the heated gum they cover the equator of the stone and take around it one or two turns of the pliant withe, securing its junction with a thong of the bark of the *courajong* tree; they then fill that part of the handle secured around the stone with the melted gum, and the weapon is ready for duty in a few hours. By the aid of this instrument the natives chop notches for the toes in ascending high trees, cut out the opossum, or tap the trees for honey; with it they also fashion wad. dies, boomerangs, and other wooden implements, and crack the bones of animals for the marrow. In some portions of the island, sinews from the tail of the kangaroo do duty as lashings. The sinews are steeped in hot water, pounded between stones to separate them into filaments, and, while yet pliable, they are wrapped around the stone and the handle; in drying they shrink and hold the objects together with great firmness. The lashing is then covered with the "black-boy gum" of the grass-tree.

The *celt* or stone axe is one of the most common objects in museums, and generally shows its adaptation to a withe handle.[72] In the excavations at Hissarlik, at a depth of from 23 to 33 feet below the present surface, Dr. Schliemann recovered well-made axes of diorite and of hard and semi-transparent greenstone.[73] One of these was fractured at the eye, but they were generally adapted for withe handles. So common is the *celt* that it has entered into the superstitions of various nations, and is supposed to be a "thunder stone"[74] and to have fallen from the sky. This idea is prevalent in China, England, India, Brittany, Finland, Japan, Brazil, Madagascar, and elsewhere.

Axes of the second class, lashed to a seat on the handle, had numerous representations at the Exhibition. Fig. 39 is a stone designed to be mounted as an adze, and Fig. 40 shows a greenstone blade lashed to a handle formed of a limb with a portion of the adjacent trunk. The fastening is evidently but a substitute for the original elaborate lashing, which had fallen off. Some of the Maori adzes are of green jade. Another stone, locally known as *toke*, is also used, but is much inferior to the former in quality and appearance. Cf. black basalt adzes found in

[71] "Aborigines of Victoria," Melbourne, 1878, i, pp. 359-380. Figs. 175-198.
[72] Dr. Abbott, in Smithsonian Report, 1875. Figs. 11, 19.
[73] Schliemann's "Troy and its Remains," p. 21, No. 2; p. 94, No. 56.
[74] Tylor's "Early History of Mankind," pp. 208, 210-211, 222-227.

Scania, Sweden,[75] and at Nootka Sound; also, the flint axes of Scandinavia, which are never bored, but are rough chipped and unground.[76]

Axes of diorite, greenstone, and basalt have sometimes holes bored through, by which to suspend them.

Fig. 41 is a stone adze (*koipele kainoa*) from

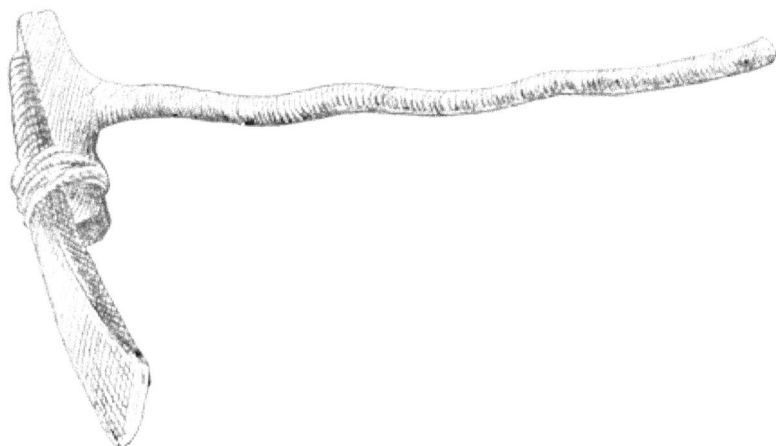

Fig. 39.—*Stone adze (unmounted), New Zealand.*

the Sandwich Islands; it is nine inches long. Fig. 42 is a shell adze from a shell heap on Saint John's River, Florida. The adze of the Pelew Islanders[77] is made of the shell of the giant clam. Shell is used as a

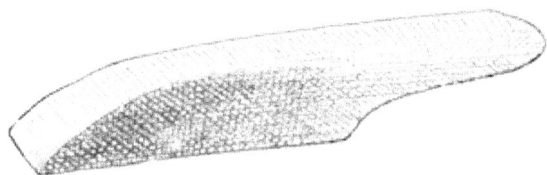

Fig. 40.—*Maori adze, New Zealand.*

material for cutting instruments in many places where stone and metal are rare; such as were formerly some of the West Indies and some islands of Polynesia and Oceanica. The Pelew Island implement may be turned

Fig. 41.—*Stone adze, Sandwich Islands.*

Fig. 42.—*Shell adze, Saint John's River, Florida.*

in the head so as to be used as an axe or an adze. The same adaptability may be found in an iron axe-adze of the Dyak of Borneo. The war axe

[75] Nilson's "Stone Age," Pl. vii, Figs. 147, 150, and page 62.

[76] *Ibid.*, p. 64, and Pl. vii, Fig. 153.

[77] Wood's "Natural History of Man," ii, p. 450.

of the Fijians is shown in Fig. 43. It was exhibited in the Main Building. Its stone head is carefully lashed with braided sinnet to an elaborately carved wooden handle.

The stone adzes of the Marquesas are most accurately shaped and
finished, especially
those of a ceremo-
nial character.
The handles of
such are fairly hon-
eycombed with
carvings, in such
a manner that a
central handle ap-
pears to be sur-
rounded by a sort

FIG. 43.—Fiji war axe.

of filigree or incrustation of geometrical work. The lashings of plaited
coir (sinnet) are very elaborate and carefully laid. Specimens obtained
by the Wilkes Expedition are in the National Museum of Washington,
D. C.

The stone adze (Fig. 44) of the Makah Indians of Puget's Sound,
California, shows an observation of the
tools of the white man. The handle is
evidently copied from that of a hand-

FIG. 44.—Stone adze, Puget's Sound.   FIG. 45.—Eskimo ice-pick. Nunivak Island

saw which the native mechanic had seen and admired. The use of the
stone and the method of lashing are, however, quite characteristic. Fig.
45 is an ice-pick of walrus ivory, lashed to a handle of pine. It is from
the Magemut Eskimo of Nunivak
Island. Fig. 46 is an Eskimo ice-
pick made from a whale's rib,
lashed with raw-hide-thongs to a
massive yew-wood handle. These
picks are used for breaking the
crust of snow and in keeping the
seal-holes open. The specimen
is from Anderson River, British
America. The example (Fig. 47)
shows another variation in the
mode of fastening. Like the

FIG. 46.—Eskimo ice-pick, British Columbia.

former, it is made from a whale's rib, and is lashed with raw-hide thongs

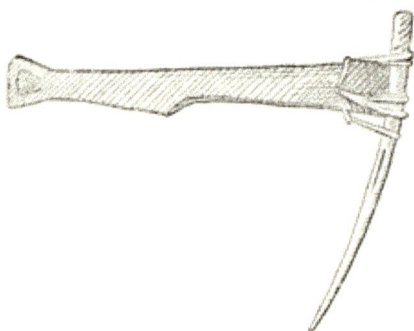

to a pine handle.   It is from the *chook chees* (*Tschuck-tschis*) of Northeast Siberia.   The mode of fastening is much like that of the old Egyptian hoes, as shown in Wilkinson's works.

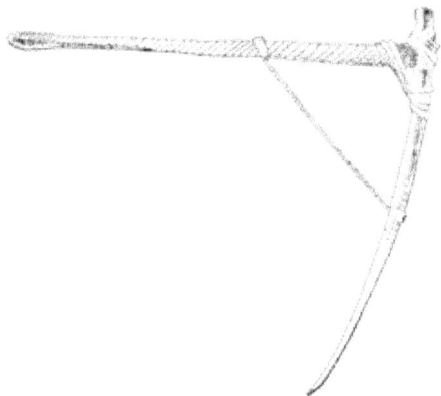

FIG. 47.—*Ice-pick and skin-dresser, Siberia.*

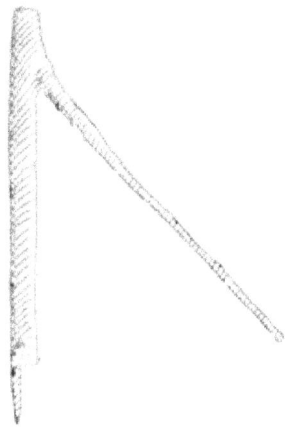

FIG. 48.—*Stone adze, British Columbia.*

Fig. 48 is the last illustration we shall offer of this mode of attaching the bit or blade to the handle of wood.   It is a small adze of argillite lashed with twisted sinews to a handle formed of a forked branch.   Such implements were used in smoothing the insides of canoes.   The main stem was grasped by the left hand, and the smaller one by the right. It is from the Haidah Indians of Bella-Bella, British Columbia.

We reach the third class of our first division and notice the single instance in the Philadelphia Exhibition in which a modern stone axe was inserted through a hole in the handle.   This has been deemed the characteristic African method, and with much reason, though instances of its adoption are found elsewhere ; the New Caledonians, for instance, mount their axes like the Africans, putting the tang of the bit through a perforated knob on the end of the handle.   As almost all the African tribes use iron, smelted and worked by native smiths, the instances of the African method will occur more frequently in the second division of the subject, which treats of metal.

The modern axe of greenstone (Fig. 49) is used in Mozambique, a Portuguese colony in

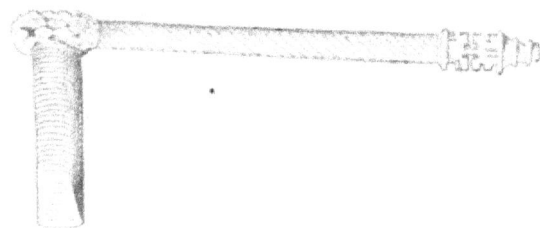

FIG. 49.—*Stone axe of Mozambique.*

Eastern Africa.   The bit is 8 inches long, and is lashed with strips of raw-hide to a wooden handle, which is carved at the hand-hold.   The lashing is covered with cowrie-shells, which form in part the currency of the natives ; they answer, we may suppose, the same purpose as the gold mounting of a dress-sword.   The inhabitants, though well acquainted with metal, retain old habits, and among them the use of stone implements, in ceremonial uses perhaps, rather than in the business of life. That stone should linger after the advent of metal is not surprising when we reflect that the stone battle-axe was used by many of the Anglo-Saxons at Hastings, and some of the Germans were armed with it at so late a period as the "Thirty Years' War."

FIG. 50.—*Stone axe.*

Fig. 50 shows one of the articles generally catalogued as a "spade-like implement." It was possibly an axe adapted to pass through the handle and be secured by a lashing of sinew or raw-hide.

Fig. 51 shows five ancient implements obtained in various parts of the United States, from mounds and elsewhere; *a*, *b*, and *d* are from Louisiana; *c* is from Iowa; *e* not noted.

The three last examples are double-headed ceremonial axes, and do not materially differ from examples in the figure following, excepting in not being perforated for the handle. The frequency of the omission indicates that the two methods of mounting were simultaneously employed.

This brings us to the fourth class—perforated axes, which are considered by Sir John Lubbock as probably characteristic of the early metallic period in Europe.[78]

It was long thought that the perforation of the axe-head did not occur until the implement came to be made of metal. It is true that the labor of boring in stone without the aid of metal and the weakening of so frangible a material might exclude that mode of mounting; but it must be recollected that time is of no moment to a savage, never having read Solomon or Dr. Watts, and not taking lessons from insects—

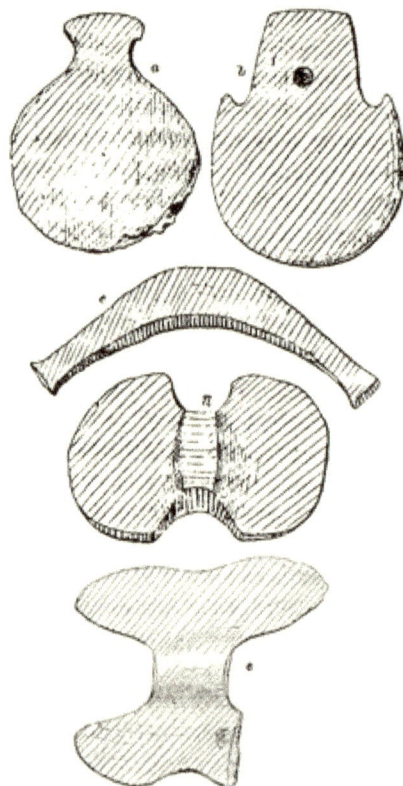

FIG. 51.—*Axes from Indian mounds, &c.*

which are simply a nuisance and point no moral in Africa.

The examples of perforated stone axes at Philadelphia (Fig. 52) were from various parts of the United States, and were shown in the Na-

<hr>

[78] Lubbock's Introduction to Nilson's "Stone Age," xxix.

tional Museum in the Government Building. They are ancient and are generally supposed to be of a ceremonial character. It was either not noted or was not observed where *a* was from ; *b, d,* and *g* were from Wisconsin ; *c* from New Jersey ; *e* from Connecticut ; *h* from Pennsylvania. So the practice of making the perforated *bipennis* in stone was widely spread. It may be mentioned that the hole in *h*, Fig. 52, is only rudimentary. A fine selection of perforated axe-heads from Denmark is in the Peabody Museum, Cam-

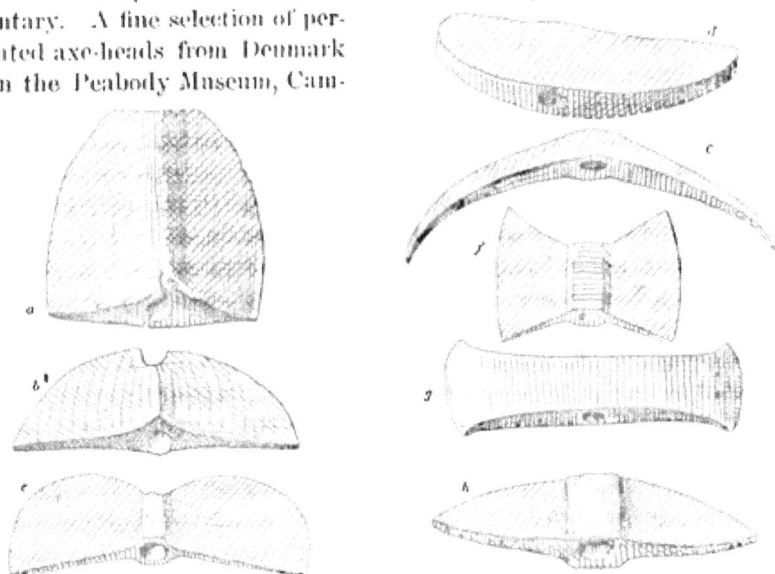

Fig. 52.—*Double-bitted perforated axes.*

bridge, and a great many more at St. Germain, France, and in the museum of Geneva, Switzerland. This object is called a "banner stone" in Abbott's article on the Stone Age in New Jersey[79]; compare also Nilson's "Stone Age."[80]

The *bipennis*, or double-bitted axe, was the weapon of the female warriors of Scythian race known as Amazons. It was also known in Assyria. Its antiquity may also be assumed from its being the sacrificial axe of the Roman priesthood: *Dolabra pontificalis.* The old *secna* or *sacena* of the Latins had two cutting edges, large and small, the former *securis ;* the latter *dolabra.* It may have been copied from the agricultural axe *dolabra*, which was something like our mattock, with an axe edge and a pick on the respective ends of the head, and was used in cutting wood and clearing land of bushes and grubs. The *dolabella* was the small axe or bill-hook. The sacrificial *malleus* was a round ball perforated for a handle, and it also seems to indicate the long-sustained use of very primitive forms of weapons and implements for ceremonial purposes.

Many copper battle-axes were recovered by Schliemann from a depth of 28 feet in the ruins of Hissarlik.[81]

[79] Smithsonian Report, 1875, p. 532.
[80] Nilson, Pl. viii, Fig. 173 and p. 71.
[81] "Troy and its Remains."

We have now reached the second division of axes, those of metal.   In this section we can scarcely preserve the quadripartite subdivisions of the stone group.   The collection, however, furnished good specimens of crude workmanship in two classes of axes— those which are lashed to a seat on a handle and those which perforate the handle.

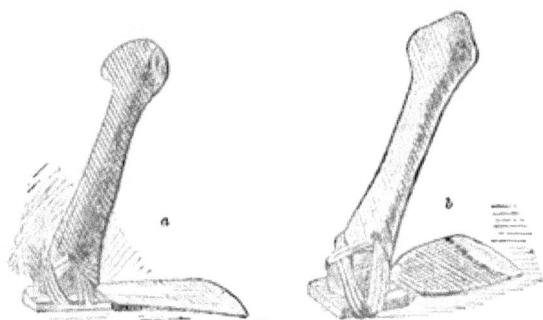

Fig. 53.—Eskimo adzes.

The examples of those which are lashed to a seat on the handle are, singularly enough, tools in which iron blades obtained from the whites have been attached to handles in the manner previously adopted with stone tools.   Fig. 53 shows two adzes of the Anderson River Eskimo, the handles of which have been ingeniously fashioned to fit the hand.   The blades are both made of hatchet heads, in one case (*a*) the eye is made use of in lashing the handle to the iron; in the other case (*b*) the eye has been ground away, and it is secured to the handle by thongs in the manner of a stone celt.   The tools indicate both the inveterate habit of mounting and also the preference for the adze method of using.

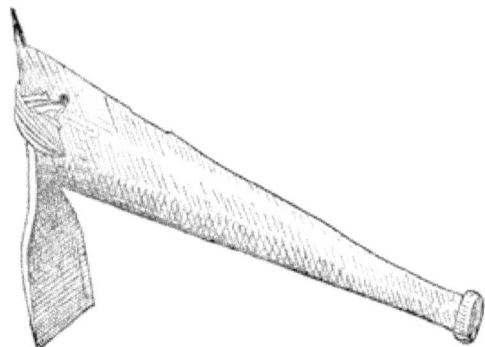

Fig. 54.—Greenlanders' adze.

The Greenlander's adze (Fig. 54), shown in the Danish department of the Main Building, is made of a common 2½-inch chisel strapped by a seal-skin thong to a beech wood handle about a foot long.   Fig. 55 is a small hand adze or chisel with a bone handle.   The blade was originally a hatchet of which the eye has been split and a piece removed.   The handle shows an imitation of a saw-handle.   It is from the Haidah Indians of Bella-Bella, British Columbia.

Fig. 55.—Indian adze, Haidahs, British Columbia.

The Javan axes[20] are mounted in different ways; two kinds, known respectively as *petel* and *wadung*, are chisel-shaped tools lashed to stocks whose natural growth as a fork facilitates that method; another, called

[20] Raffles "Java," 4to, i, 174, Figs. 1, 2, 4.

sang'luk; has an eye for the helve in the manner next in order to be considered.

The Javan battle-axe (*kudi tranchang*), formerly a principal weapon of Java,[83] is not now much used, and is suprisingly like a freakish weapon used by the natives of Central Africa.

The Japanese axe is a compromise, its bent tang being held by a ring which slips on the handle.[84]

Africa furnishes us with the greatest variety of the axes which perforate the handle. Beginning at the south, we find the Kafirs[85] in possession of an axe, but their principal weapon is the

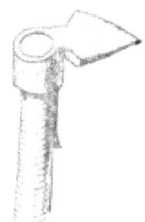

Fig. 56.—*Japanese axe.*

Fig. 57.—*Bechuana axes, South Africa.*

assegai, a javelin made by their native blacksmiths. With the *keerie* or short club, shield, and assegais, a Zulu considers himself well furnished.

The Bechuana axe, Fig. 57, is a steel bit simply fastened by a tang in the enlarged wooden head. The term Bechuana may be used generally to include a number of tribes, embracing the Makololo,[86] who are among the most accomplished workers in metal on the continent.

The smaller axes in Fig. 57 are other patterns, made by the Bechuanas; and Fig. 58 is a still more fanciful one, shown in the Portuguese Colonies Department of

Fig. 58.—*Battle-axe, Angola, Africa.*

the Agricultural Building. The head is of steel and the handle is in part wrapped with fine wire. The blade is peculiar in form and ornamentation, and has what we should consider a rather insecure attachment to the helve. Fig. 59 is another axe of Angola, shown in the same collection; it has a curious curved blade and a long tang inserted in the

Fig. 59.—*Axe of Angola.*

usual African method into the wooden handle.

The elephant axe of the Banyai,[87] of the Zambesi, was also snown in

[83] Raffles "Java," 4to, i, Pl. opp. p. 296, Fig. 7.

[84] Siebold's "Nippon," vi, Pl. 6; also ii, Pl. 5 *bis.*, Figs. 14, 9, 15, 16, 13; also ii, Pl. 11, 13.

[85] Casalis' "Basutos," 132.　[86] Baines' "South Africa," 467.　[87] Wood i, p. 404.

the group of Angola and Mozambique weapons, Fig. 60.   It has a very long tang projecting entirely through the handle, and secured thereto by raw-hide lashing.   One end has an axe-blade and the other a spear point.   The handle is made by cutting off a limb of a convenient length, and also a small piece of the trunk at the insertion of the branch.   A hole for the tang is then bored through the knotty wood, where the limb is as it were rooted into the body of the tree.   The handle is then dressed to shape. The blade is sometimes three feet in length, and is carried over the shoulder.   It is used in ham-stringing the elephant.   The hunters go in pairs, one carrying the axe while the other goes before the animal to distract his attention.   The axeman comes up behind stealthily and severs one ham-string of the animal at a single blow.   One form of the elephant axe was noticed to have a curved handle and a stay-lashing at a point six inches distant from the socket.

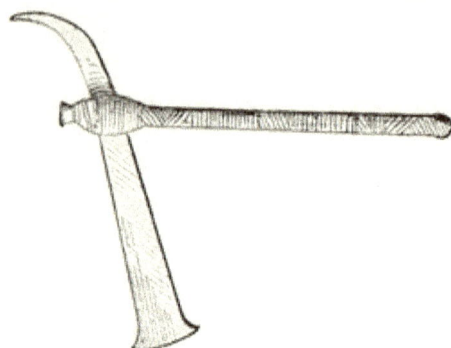

FIG. 60.— *Elephant axe of the Banyai, Zambesi, Africa.*

The Banyai of the Zambesi have also a convertible axe and adze.   The knob of the handle has two slits at right angles, so that the tang of the blade may be optionally inserted either to bring the edge in line with the sweep of the tool, as with the axe, or transversely, as with the adze.   Curiously enough the Water Dyaks, of Borneo, have a chipping tool of the same kind used in boat-building.[58]   It has an iron blade, wooden head, and ratan (Malay *rôtan*) lashing.   The blade has a square tang, and by taking it out of the socket, turning it one-quarter round, and inserting it again the blade is changed, in reference to the handle, from an axe to an adze, or *vice versa.*

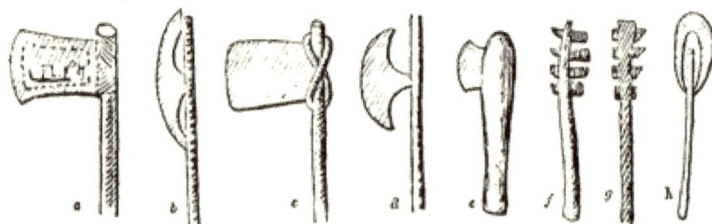

FIG. 61.—*Axes of Egypt, India, Mexico, and Yucatan.*

The Djibba axe has two pointed prongs projecting lengthwise from the head to make it efficient in thrusting.   The Monbuttoo axe,[59] following the universal African type, has its tang inserted through the thick end of a knobbed club.

---

[58] Wood, vol. ii, p. 453.   [59] Schweinfurth's "Africa," vol. ii, p. 112.

Fig. 61 shows that this system of inserting the blade in the handle has been practiced in far distant times and places. *a b* are ancient forms of Egyptian bronze axes.[20] *c d* are ancient axes from the Sachi tope[21] at Bhilsa, in Central India. *e* is an axe shown on a Mexican monument. The obsidian or copper blade is inserted in the handle. *f* and *g* show the instrument known as *mahquahuitl*, a double-headed axe with obsidian

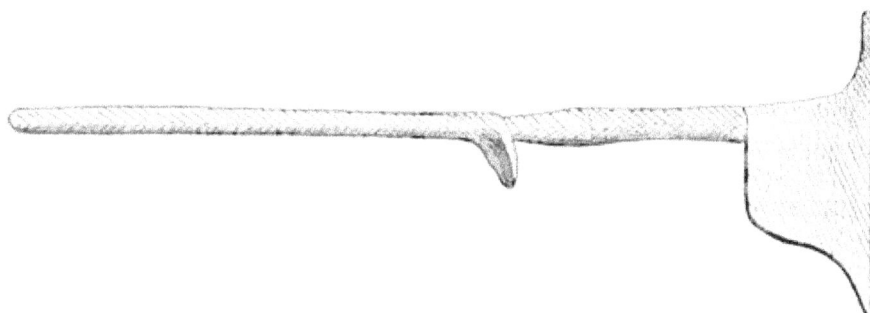

FIG. 62.—*Axe of the Philippines.*

flakes inserted in wooden handles. *h* shows a copper axe of Yucatan, the plate being inserted in a slitted handle. The battle-axe was the weapon of the Peru-vian soldiery.[22] Nu-merous Trojan battle-axes of copper were found by Dr. Schlie-mann at Hissarlik.[23]

The axe of the Phil-ippines was shown in the Spanish Building. It has a peculiarly shaped head and a long

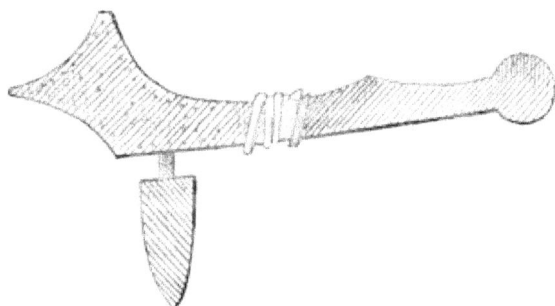

FIG. 63.—*Casse-tête, Dakotah.*

ferrule. The hand-stop on the helve was the only instance of the kind in the exhibition. It is a sort of rudimentary guard, like a partial hilt on the two-handed helve. (Fig. 62.)

The jungle hook of the Singhalese (*wal-dakat*) and a chopping axe (*proa*)[24] are used for clearing brush and cutting trees. Even the poor Veddahs of the interior forests "have a little ax, which they stick in by their sides, to cut honey out of hollow trees."[25]

Fig. 63 is a Dakotah Indian war-club (*casse-tête*) ornamented with carving and armed with a leaf-shaped steel point. The peasant of Brit-tany carries a knobbed stick resembling the *Kafir knob-keerie*. (Fig. 1.)

[20] Kitto, vol. i, p. 507; "Daleth," p. 7.
[21] Cunningham's "Bhilsa Tope," pl. xv, Figs. 8, 9.
[22] Prescott's "Conquest of Peru," vol. i, p. 72.
[23] Schliemann's "Troy and its Remains," pp. 330, 331.
[24] Knox's "Ceylon," pp. 273–4.
[25] *Ibid.*, p. 61.

It is called a *casse-tête* by the French of the neighboring departments, but *pen-bas* by the Bretons.[96] See also the marble knob for a stick, found by Dr. Schliemann at Ilium.[97]

The same form is shown by Catlin to have been very common among the Blackfeet and other Indian tribes on the headwaters of the Missouri. An axe of Terra del Fuego, shown by Nilson, has a blade of iron inserted in the African manner in a wooden stock which has been dressed by flint tools.[98] Desor also shows hatchets of diorite, serpentine, and quartzite in sockets of buckhorn, which were mounted in a wooden handle by a lateral hole in the side of the club. In another case the stone was inserted endwise in a horn socket which was pierced for the handle.[99] In another case the stone in a horn handle had the position formerly occupied by the brow antler.

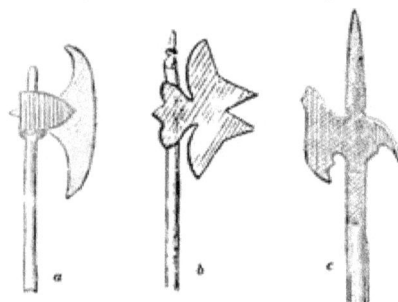

Fig. 64 — *Halberds, India and Norway.*

Fig. 65 — *Norwegian axes.*

Fig. 66 — *Iron tomahawk, Dakotah.*

Fig. 64 shows three forms of halberds, light axes on long handles: *c* is from Norway and belongs to the class with a tang driven into the handle; *a b* are Sowrah battle-axes from India, and belong to the last class of our list—the handle inserted through an eye in the head. To this also belong the Norwegian axes (Fig. 65) and the Arickaree iron tomahawk (Fig. 66).

III.—KNIVES AND SWORDS.

The knife in its primitive form is a sharp flake of stone or obsidian, a sliver of bamboo or wood, or a shell with a sharpened edge. When the point is the specially engaged portion the weapon is a dagger. Many other crude materials furnish the hand-to-hand cutting or piercing weapons, such as the pointed horns of animals, the tail of the sting-ray,

---

[96] Trollope's "Summer Tour in Brittany," London, 1840, Pls. opp. pp. 125, 220, 296.
[97] Schliemann's "Troy and its Remains," p. 265.
[98] "Stone Age," Pl. vii, Fig. 155.
[99] Desor. transl. in Smithsonian Report, 1865, pp. 360, 361, Figs. 17, 18, 19.

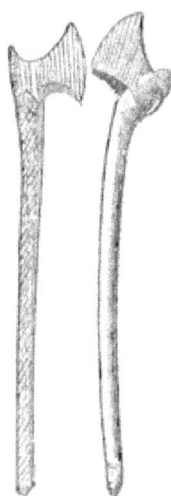

shark's teeth tied upon a staff, and sharpened bones. When the disposition exists a weapon will be found somewhere, and the most curious are those where the choice of material is but small and metal is inaccessible. Metal once obtained, the variety of weapons decreases, and knives, daggers, and swords assume a somewhat uniform character.

The persistent ceremonial use of stones for knives, after the use of metal had been fully established for the ordinary affairs of life, is noticeable in many old records and in the observation of late travelers. We may mention the stone knives used by the Egyptians, Ethiopians, and Hebrews in circumcision,[100] by the Egyptians in embalming,[101] in obtaining the balm of Gilead,[102] in the human sacrifices of Mexico, in the gashing of the flesh of fanatics,[103] and in inducing the cicatrized wounds which form the ornaments or tribal marks of some savages. To these may be added the gashing of the flesh by the New Zealanders in their mourning, and the stone fleams used by the North American Indians for bleeding.

Museums have crude stone spalls and well-fashioned knives of stone in variety, but we can only appeal for illustrations to the collection in Philadelphia. In the upper and stone periods of the hill of Hissarlik in Asia

Fig. 67.—Obsidian nucleus and flakes, Mexico.

Minor, Schliemann found numerous flint knives.[104] Some have edges like ordinary knives; others are serrated. At a depth of 23 feet he found double-edged knives of obsidian, sharp as razors.

Fig. 68.—Obsidian knife, California.

Flint flakes and nuclei from the stone age of Scandinavia, and flint knives from Greenland and New Zealand made of spalls, and others of chipped flint, are shown by Nilson[105] and by Dr. Abbott, of New Jersey.[106]

Obsidian was a favorite material where obtainable. It was used in Mexico in the manufacture of sacrificial flake-knives, arrow-points, &c.[107] The flakes were split off by the skillfully applied pressure of a T-shaped wooden implement. The nucleus and flakes (Fig. 67) were shown in the National Museum and are from Mexico. The same collection in the Government Building had the obsidian knife (Fig. 68). This has a

[100] Exodus, iv, 25; Joshua, v, 2.
[101] Herodotus, ii, 86; Diodorus Siculus, i, 91; Kitto, i, 81.
[102] Pliny, xii, 54.
[103] Ibid., xxxv, 46; xi, 109. Compare also Pliny, xix, 57; xxiii, 81; xxiv, 6, 62.
[104] "Troy and its Remains," p. 79.
[105] "Stone Age," p. 76 and Pl. ii; Figs. 24, 23, and Pl. iii, v.
[106] Smithsonian Report, 1875, p. 300.
[107] Torquemada.

wooden handle which shows the marks of a similar cutting instrument, and is therefore a veritable specimen of the stone age.

The Yellowstone Park has lately been stated to possess hills of obsidian of different colors, which have afforded for ages the material for the arrow-heads of the Indian tribes in the vicinity.

The flint knives of the Indians of the California peninsula are mentioned by Baegert.[108]

As far away as the Admiralty Islands of the Papuan group we find obsidian used for knives, razors, and spear-points.[109] The natives tie the spear-heads to the shaft with plaited string coated with gum. The knife used by the New Caledonians for carving the human body is called *nbouet*, and is a flat serpentine stone oval in form and seven inches in length. Holes are bored in it, by which it is fastened to a wooden handle. The New Caledonians eat their slain enemies, the women, who are the cooks, following the army and dragging the bodies off the field to prepare them for the supper of their returning husbands and brothers. The palms being considered as tid-bits, are the perquisites of the priests. Each part belongs to certain persons, and the carving is regulated by rules. The body is opened by the *nbouet* and the intestines removed with a fork made of two human arm bones sharply pointed and lashed together. The women cooks prefer to truss the bodies in sitting posture, bake them whole, and serve them in war costume.

Many collections show knives of flakes of silex mounted in wooden and horn backs,[110] and serrated knives or saws made by the insertion of flakes of obsidian, flint, or shark's teeth in a grooved wooden back. Some are mentioned later when referring to spears. Such are found in California, Sweden, the Philippines, Australia, and elsewhere. The knife[111] *dabba* of the Victorian blacks consists of quartz fragments attached to a wooden handle with gum.

Passing to knives of wood, we find none which would make impressive illustrations; in the South Sea islands wood has been the principal material; until lately stone was unknown in some islands, and metal in almost all. The Fijian knife for cutting up *bakolo* (long pig), as the edible human body is called, was a sharp sliver of bamboo.[112] The Ajitas of the Philippines and New Guineans also use the bamboo sliver.[113] The Sandwich Islanders have a battledore-shaped piece of wood[114], like the *merai* of the Maories, but armed on the edge with shark's teeth. It was formerly employed in cutting up the bodies of warriors who fell in battle, or of persons sacrificed. The Mundurucus of the Amazon use a

[108] Translation in Smithsonian Report, 1863, p. 363.
[109] Wood, vol. ii, p. 302.
[110] Desor. transl. in Smithsonian Report, 1865, p. 360.
[111] Smith's "Aborigines of Victoria."
[112] Smythe's "Ten Months in Fiji," p. 85.
[113] Wood, vol. ii, p. 242.
[114] *Ibid.*, vol. ii, p. 435.

bamboo knife in decapitating their enemies to prepare the heads as trophies. The gentle savages are, however, not oblivious of the value of
metal when they have an opportunity to see it. Francis Sparrow, whom
Raleigh left to explore the country of the Orinoco, received eight beau-
tiful young women for a red-handled knife—value in England at that
time equal to one cent.

The Australian dagger is a stick pointed at both ends, grasped by the
midlength, and struck right and left.[115]

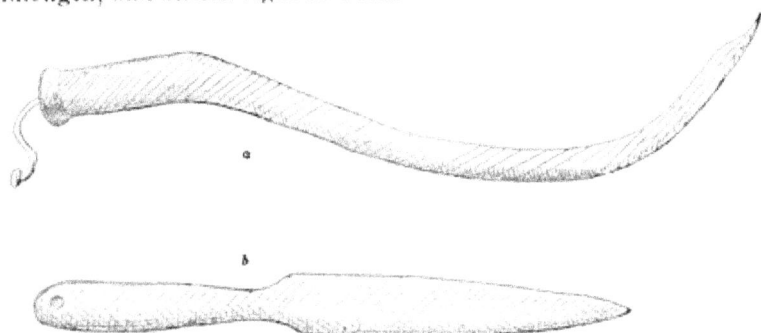

Fig. 69.—Greenlanders' bone knives.

In the extreme northern countries no material is so ready to hand as
bone. The harpoons, knives, and many other domestic implements of the
Eskimo are of bone. Fig. 69 shows the fish and blubber knives of the
Kajak natives of Greenland. They were shown in the Danish collection
in the Main Building. *a* is made of the bone of a whale, and is 18 inches
long; *b* is of wood, and is 10 inches long. Fig. 70 shows two other bone
implements of the Kajaks, a bone knife used in skinning the seal, and
a fish scoop. The knife is 14 inches long and two and a half inches wide;
the bone spoon is four inches long and two wide.

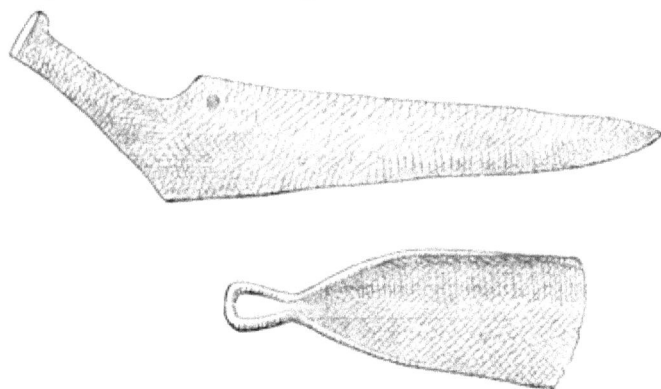

Fig. 70.—Bone implements of Greenland.

Some of the bone knives of the Laplanders are very elaborate, especially those used in preparing skins.

[115] Smith's "Aborigines of Victoria," vol. i, p. 302.

The Eskimo in winter live in dome-shaped houses, called *igloos*, built of blocks of ice or snow. These blocks are *roussoir* shaped, so that they make a safe and symmetrical vaulted structure. They are hewn from the bank or field of solidified snow with large knives like Fig. 71,

Fig. 71.—*Eskimo bone snow-knife.*

made of the bones of whales. Several of these knives were shown in the National Museum and in the Greenland department of the Danish collection. Two men, one to cut blocks and one to lay them, will erect a house in two hours. Just above the door a large plate of fresh-water ice is built in so as to illuminate the interior. Inside is a raised bench of snow, on which are laid sprigs and such scanty vegetation as the summer affords, to support the seal-skins which form the bed and bench. The dwellings are sometimes as much as 16 feet in diameter and 8 feet in height. The inevitable lamp is a stone dish with a wick of moss supported in it, and a quantity of oil fed from blubber piled upon it. This lamp is at once the warming and cooking stove, the light, the means of drying the clothes and melting the snow for drink, for the whole family occupying the *igloo*. Above the lamp is the cooking-pot, which also does duty in containing snow to be melted for drinking water. Above the cooking-pot (and by this time we are pretty near the roof) is a net spread to hold wet fur clothes, in order that they may be dried; after which they are chewed to make them supple.

Poniards and pike-heads of bones of deer and urus are described by Desor.[116]

One or two other instances of animal material used in knives and daggers may be mentioned before we reach the metallic. The double dagger of the East Indies has two sharpened antelope horns joined at their bases; or it is a single straight two-ended blade of steel, a circular guard protecting the handle of the weapon, which is intended to strike right and left in a crowd. The Sandwich Islanders use daggers (*pahúa*) of wood, held in the middle and having a point at each end. The large mussel shell is the knife of the Fuegian; the original edge is knocked off and the solid portion made sharp by grinding upon a stone. The dagger of the Pelew Islanders is the tail bone of the sting-ray, and it is carried in a sheath formed of a joint of bamboo. The Tahitian dagger has the tail of the sting-ray as a point; it comes off in the wound and works deeper and deeper.

Fig. 72.—*Indian knife of native copper.*

This brings us to metal, of which we first consider copper.
The copper knife, Fig. 72, was taken from an Indian mound. It does

116 Desor. Translation in Smithsonian Report, 1865, p. 358.

not appear that any of the North American Indians who had access to copper worked it by smelting; but they treated it as malleable stone and shaped it by hammering. The Greenland Eskimo make knives from the copper obtained from Coppermine River, from flint, from walrus ivory, or from such pieces of iron as they may obtain by barter or may pick up from whalers or explorers.

Fig. 73 shows a number of copper implements—knives, a spear, and

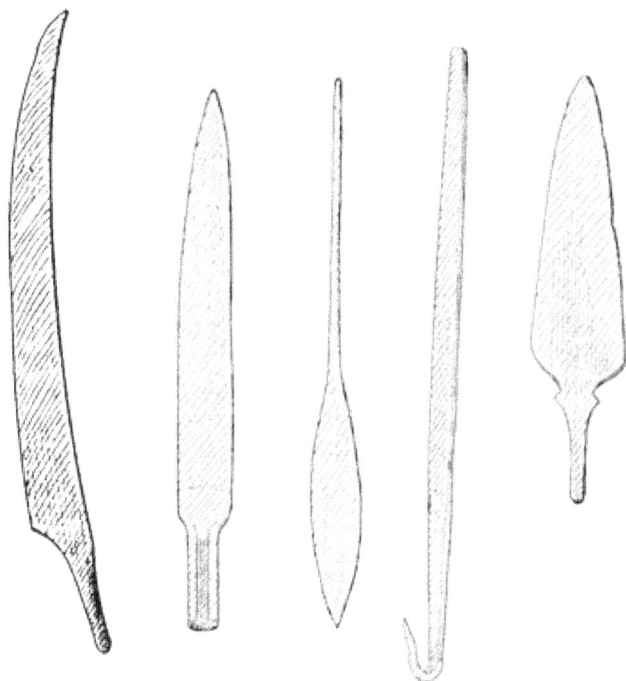

FIG. 73.—*Native copper implements, Wisconsin.*

a hook; these are Indian remains from Wisconsin, the metal having doubtless been obtained from the Lake Superior copper district in earlier times. They, together with many other copper tools, were exhibited by the Wisconsin Historical Society in the Mineral Annex of the Main Building. We cannot pretend to distinguish carefully between the weapon and the domestic implement. A knife is a knife whether for the throat of an enemy or of a deer.

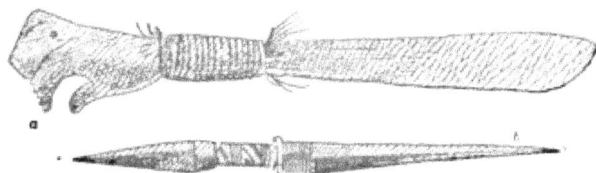

FIG. 74.—*Copper weapon and steel dagger, British Columbia.*

Fig. 74 shows a knife-like club a of native copper, a hereditary possession in the family of a Haidah chief in British Columbia. Beneath it is shown a double-ended dagger (*b*), bound with copper, and obtained from the Kutchin Indians of Northwest British America. Such daggers are forged by the Indians from old files obtained from sawmills near the settlements. They are in general use among the northern and north-western tribes.

Copper seems to have been the earliest metal to be fashioned into tools, and its alloy, bronze, the first efficient tool material. Molds of mica schist for casting copper weapons and ornaments were found by Dr. Schliemann in the hill of Hissarlik.[117] There are also many such specimens in museums. The modern supposition that the ancients had a method of tempering copper as we do steel—or with analogous effects at least—is a myth. The metal acted upon was the alloy, bronze, and the range of effects is far inferior to the capacity of steel.

The Assyrians wore a profusion of daggers, two or more in the same sheath.[118] The handles were elaborate, made of ivory, inlaid, set with precious stones, carved the shape of heads of animals, etc. One of copper was found by Layard at Nimroud. The Assyrians, like the Persians, probably used them as knives.

Copper knives were found by Schliemann[119] in the lowest stratum of the excavations at Hissarlik; one of them was gilt. Also a number of copper daggers at a depth of 28 feet.

Egyptian knives were of bronze and of copper.[120]

A comparison of the forms of knives of the ancients and moderns shows that what may be termed the "leaf-shape" has been very general. It is true that the variety of shapes of leaves is so great that the term may be held indescriptive; it suits the case, however.

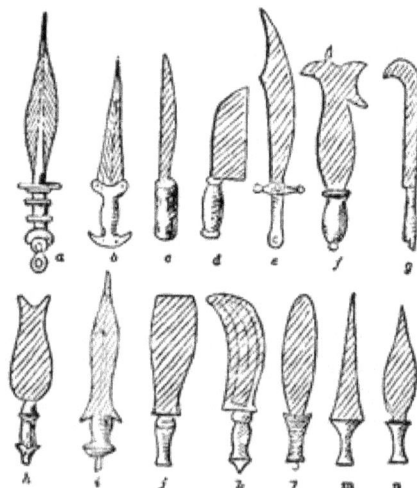

FIG. 75.—*Ancient Roman and modern African knives.*

Fig. 75 shows, in the upper row, a number of Roman knives of the classical period, and in the lower row a number of African knives of the present day. *a* is the *secespita*, a sacrificial knife with an iron blade and an ivory handle ornamented with gold and silver; *b* is the *pugio* or two-edged dagger worn by the officers of the army and by persons of rank; *c* is the *culter coquinarius*, or cook's knife; *d*, the *cultrarius*, for cutting the throat of the sacrificial victim; *e*, the *c. renatorius*, or huntsman's knife; *f*, the *falx vinitoria*, or vinedresser's knife; *g*, the *falx arboraria*, for pruning and hedge-trimming.

The swords of the bronze age, dug up from the lacustrine village

[117] Schliemann's "Troy and its Remains," p. 139.   [118] "Nineveh," vol. ii, p. 264.
[119] "Troy and its Remains," 150; pp. 332, 333.   [120] Wilkinson. Kitto, vol. i, p. 372.

sites, are many of them like some of the figures, in the upper especially.
See Desor,[121] where they are shown, some with grooved blades and as
much as 59 centimeters in length; also bronze poniards and knives with
tongs and sockets.[122]

The lower row shows h i j k, knives of the Fans of Western Africa.
These are sometimes as much as three feet in length and seven inches
in width; they are kept very sharp in a sheath of wood, which is in two
halves, and is bound together with strips of raw-hide covered with snake
or human skin.   l is an Unyoro knife of iron, the handle bound with
copper wire.[123]   m n are two two-edged daggers of the Niam-niams.[124]
The dagger is worn in a sheath of skin attached to the girdle.   The lances
knives, and daggers have blood-grooves, differing in this respect from
the Bonjo or Dyoor weapons.   Both of the last-mentioned tribes have
two-handled knives.   The Bonjo knife[125] is used by the women in peeling
tubers and slicing gourds and cucumbers; it has an oval shape, and is
sharp on both sides, like the Unyoro knife l, Fig. 75.   The Dyoor
knife[126] is spindle-shaped, and is used for similar purposes.

Dr. Schliemann found, in his excavations at Troy, a dagger of steel

four inches long.   The blade, which is double-edged and in
the form of an arrow, is 1.6 inches long, and in a perfect
state of preservation, which Dr. Schliemann attributes to
the antiseptic power of the red wood ashes,
mixed with charcoal, in which he found it em-
bedded, in the large mansion close to the gate,
28 feet below the surface.

The Balonda dagger from the Zambesi is
shown in Fig. 76, and has a remarkable resemblance to a and i, Fig. 75, which are respectively
Roman and Gaboon.   This dagger is 24 inches
long, and the handle is partly wrapped with
raw-hide.   The handle is by no means a convenient one, but no doubt the owner felt well
satisfied with its ornamental appearance as it
protruded from the scabbard.

Fig. 77 is an Angola dagger, with an iron
blade and wooden handle.   It looks much more
like business than its fellow.

Fig. 78 shows an Angola dagger, with a
strangely-shaped scabbard of sheet copper.
It has a copper-covered wooden handle and a
steel blade.   The broad base of the sheath is probably indicative of its

Fig. 76.—Dagger of Balonda, Africa.

Fig. 77.—Angola Dagger.

[121] Translation in Smithsonian Report, 1865, p. 374.
[122] Ibid., pp. 374, 371-372.
[123] Baker's "Ismailia," plate opposite p. 135.
[124] Schweinfurth's "Africa," vol. ii, pp. 10, 27.
[125] Ibid., vol. i, p. 281.
[126] Wood, vol. i, p. 503.

nationality, the same feature not having been noticed elsewhere. Its purpose is not apparent. The sheath of the *kris* has a considerable lateral enlargement at the upper end, but that weapon has a corresponding guard. It will be referred to presently, among swords.

Fig. 78.—*Angola dagger.*

The collection of savage arms from the Portuguese colonies of Angola and Mozambique, exhibited in the Agricultural Building, was not excelled in its kind in the whole Exhibition. With many additions, it was again exhibited in Paris in 1878.

Some of the articles therein shown were from the Banyai of the Zambesi, the Bechuanas, and tribes with which the parties crossing between the western and eastern coasts of the continent come in contact. Passing south and west to Natal, a very warlike people, the Zulus and Basuto Kafirs, are encountered. The articles from this people were shown in the Cape of Good Hope collection, and are noticed among clubs and spears; they do not use the bow and arrow. The *assegai* is the principal knife of the Kafir.[127] It is of semi-steel of soft temper, and will bend and keep its shape, which is taken advantage of by the natives in making bowls, spoons, and pipes. He prefers it to the steel of the white man, which breaks. The Bechuanas make the best knives in that region, and barter them to other tribes. The blade has a long lanceolate shape, with two edges, and the weapon is worn suspended from the neck.[128] The handle, of ivory or wood, is carefully carved, frequently representing an animal, a hyena or giraffe, for instance. The wooden sheath is made of two pieces of wood, hollowed out and bound together with sinews. The same is used among some tribes of Kafirs. The carving tool of the Bechuanas is more like a chisel; a blade like a thumb-nail in the end of a handle. The Japanese knives are numerous and peculiar.[129]

Fig. 79.—*Blackfoot scalping-knife.*

Fig. 79 is a leaf-shaped dagger or scalping-knife, of iron, with a bone handle, such as is used by the Blackfeet and Sioux. C. Carver, in his "Travels," says that the leaf-shaped dagger, made in his time of bone, was peculiar to the Nadowessioux, or that family later known as the Da-ko-tahs or Sioux.

There is one class of weapons for grappling at close quarters, which may be mentioned here, as it was shown in the exhibit from British India. The *baymak* is a five-clawed weapon hidden in the hand, having loops through which the first and fourth fingers are passed. When the

---

127 Wood, vol. i, p. 103.   128 Casalis' "Basutos," p. 136.

129 Siebold's "Nippon," vii, plate 19, Figs. 3, 4, 5, 6.

hand is opened, the steel claws, like those of a lion, are exposed, and are intended to rip the naked belly of the adversary. The term *baymak* is understood to include several forms of weapons, such as brass knuckles and spikes which are carried in the hand.

The Samoans have a somewhat similar weapon—a glove made of coir, and having on the inside several rows of shark's teeth, set hooking so that they retain anything which is grasped. Like the *baymak*, it is intended to rip the abdomen of an enemy. To guard themselves against this weapon the Samoans use a heavy and wide belt of coir, reaching from the arm-pits to the hips. This belt was the nearest to the nature of clothing of anything in the islands; a number of cords of sinnet are strained on two parallel sticks about 35 inches apart; the sinnet weft is then worked in over and under alternate threads.[119]

The *bague de mort*, seen by Stendhal in Rome,[120] is like the East Indian *baymak* in the mode of hiding it in the hand, but it has only two claws, which are of steel, very sharp and like those of lions. The piece to which the claws are rooted is held in the hand by rings, through which pass the second and third fingers, beneath which the claws are hidden, nothing appearing but the rings. Poison is placed in grooves channeled in the claws, like the poison groove in the fang of a rattle-snake.

Stendhal says: "Dans une foule, au bal par example, on saississait avec une apparence de galanterie la main nue de la femme dont on voulait se venger; en la serrant et retirant le bras, on la déchirait profondément, et, en même temps, on laissait tomber la *bague de mort*. Comment, dans une foule, trouver le coupable?"

The Djibba tribe of the Upper Nile wear bracelets for cutting and tearing, the edge being protected by leathern sheaths when the weapon is not required for duty. Some of them have double jagged edges and others a single sharp edge.

The Nuehr carry on the wrist an iron ring with projecting blades.

The Roman boxing gauntlet, *cestus*, was a much less sanguinary affair, being merely armed with lead or with bosses.

We pass from knives to swords; which is but to an implement of a larger kind. The sword proper is a weapon, but the machete of the Spaniard, the corn and cane knives of the plantation and farm, are domestic implements of similar character, but with less ornamental furnishing. Where vegetation is as large as that of the corn or sugar cane, a sword-like implement is necessary in gathering it, and the same large knife is used in tropical countries in cutting away the vines and creepers which obstruct the narrow passes through the woods.[121]

Of the cruder materials, stone and wood, used in swords, the Exhibition furnished but few examples. Some of the clubs already considered

---

[119] Wood, vol. ii, p. 354.

[120] "Promenades dans Rome," vol. i, p. 267.

[121] Raffle's "Java," 4to, p. 113.

had sharpened edges and approximated the sword character. The New
Zealand stone sword, Fig. 80, can hardly be classed under any other
head, as it has a handle, a back, and an edge, and is adapted to deliver a cutting blow. The swords of the
Pelew Islanders are of wood inlaid with pieces of shell.[132]
The Kingsmill Islanders have wooden swords, armed on
their edges with sharks' teeth lashed with sinnet braided
from the fiber of the cocoa-nut. The wooden blade has
grooved ridges to receive the teeth, corresponding holes being made in the
ridges and teeth through which the
braided cord is repeatedly passed to
fasten the teeth in this artificial alve-
olar ridge. The swords are single or
double edged, and have guards similarly
armed with teeth, so that no part of the
weapon except the handle can be touched
with impunity. The spears are similarly
armed, like some which were shown from
the Philippine Islands. A fine assort-
ment of those weapons, obtained by the
Wilkes Expedition, is in the National
Museum at Washington.

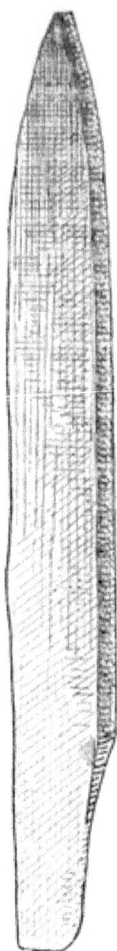

The gold-coast section of the English
colonies presented two curious swords
with broad, thin blades, especially wide
near the point. The perforations make
the blade still lighter. The tang is set
in a wooden handle with two knobs, between which is the hand-hold. Fig. 82
has a double blade, and is referred to as
an "executioner's sword"; a weapon in
much demand all around that part of
the world, especially Dahomé. The two
blades of Fig. 82 are united at a point

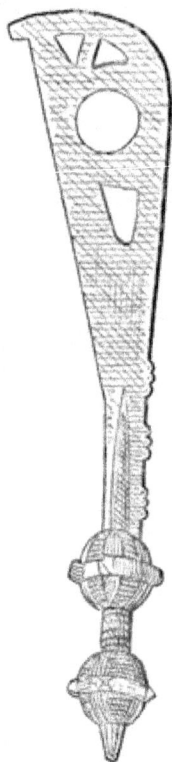

Fig. 80.—*Maori stone sword.*

Fig. 81.—*Sword of the gold coast, Africa.*

where the flattening of the blades commences. The blades are 24 inches
long; the carved handles are 8 inches long, and one of them is gilded.
The swords of Dahomé[133] have knobs on the ends of the blades, so
that they may be used as clubs. One noticed had a knob carved like a
human head. The back of another had a series of backwardly-curved
prongs, intended as hooks to catch a pursued enemy. The classic *harpe*,
the sword of Mercury and Perseus, had a similar prong, *hamus*. Another
sword of bloody renown is the weapon of the "Razor Women," who form

---

[132] Wood, vol. i, p. 449.
[133] Duncan's "Western Africa," p. 226.

one battalion of the Dahomé Amazons.   The weapon is copied from the white man's razor, but has a blade 2 feet long, and a handle of proportionate size.   A spring holds the blade open.   It is as if, in a jocular spirit, some trader had foisted an absurdity upon them; but the natives claim it as an invention of the late King Gezo.   The real razor of the Ashantee is of a nearly trapezoidal form; this latter is for legitimate shaving.

Coming southwardly along the coast of Africa we arrive at Angola, which, as we have already had occasion to remark, was well represented in the Agricultural Building. Fig. 83 is a sword made by a native armorer of Angola; it has a curiously-shaped hilt, and tufts of horse-hair stained red. The hilt is in part covered with sheet-lead. The gay appearance of the hilt, as it showed when sheathed and worn at the side, was probably its principal recommendation. The general shape of the African sword is curved, although of the examples from the Portuguese colonies two are straight and but one bent.   The specimens illustrated from other sections of the continent will amply compensate for the present larger majority of straight-bladed weapons.   Fig. 84 shows a native sword of Mozambique.   It has a short wooden handle, from which the usual button on the end of the tang has dropped off.   The guard of the hilt has a peculiar scroll shape, and one branch has been broken.   The sword of the Hamram Arabs, of Central Africa,[124] is also straight, double-edged, and has a cross-guard.   The blade is 36 inches long, and each edge is as sharp as a razor.   It is carried in a wooden scabbard made of two pieces, hollowed to receive the blade, and covered with leather. With this weapon the Arab will cut a man in two, or will hamstring an elephant.

FIG. 82.—Two-bladed sword of the gold coast, Africa.

FIG. 83.—Sword of Angola, Africa.

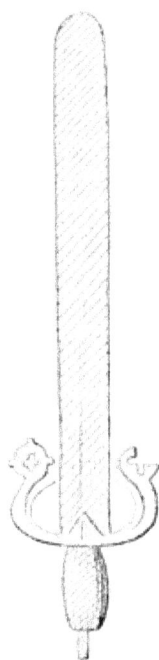

FIG. 84.—Sword of Mozambique, Africa.

Fig. 85 is a steel cimeter of Mozambique, with a broad and very thin blade. It has a wooden handle ornamented with sheet brass enchased and jeweled. It is 40 inches long, and has a groove near the back of the blade.

Fig. 86 is a sickle-shape cimeter, brought by Col. Long (Bey) on his return from his expedition into Central Africa in the service of the Khedive. It was shown in the Egyptian Department in the Main Building, and is like the weapon represented by Schweinfurth as held by the Monbuttoo King Munza during the audience which he held with that potentate.[135]

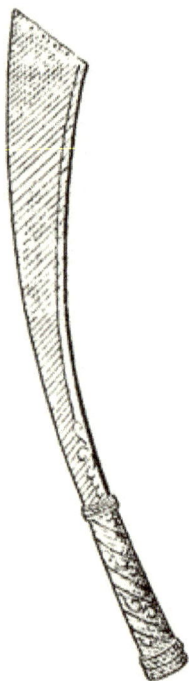

Fig. 85.—Cimeter of Mozambique, Africa.

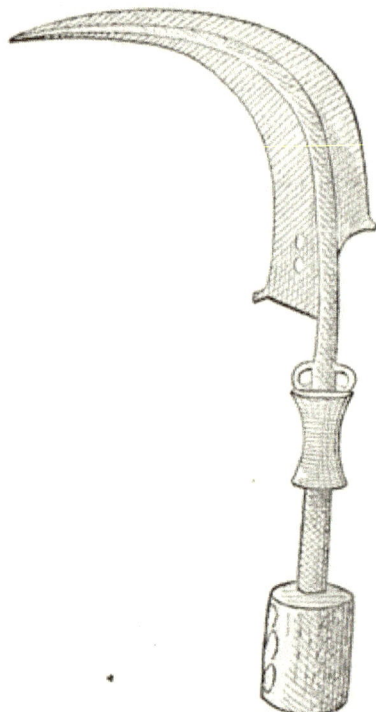

Fig. 86.—Monbuttoo cimeter, Central Africa.

It is usually of steel, but on that occasion was a weapon of ceremony, and made of pure copper. The adjacent tribe, the Niam-niams, use implements of somewhat similar shape, curved broad-ended blades, somewhat after the bill-hook order, reminding one of the corresponding Roman implement, the *falx vinitoria*.

The *kookery* of the Ghoorkas, a tiger-fighting hill tribe of India,[136] is another example of a boldly curved chopping-sword, broad near the end, and sharpened on the concave edge, which is, however, of an ogee shape. It is about fifteen inches long, is used either to cut or thrust, and is made of the famous "Wootz" steel. Two little knives are carried in side pockets of the scabbard.

135 "Africa," vol. ii, pp. 9, 10, 107.   136 Wood, vol. ii, p. 760.

Fig. 87 is a saber brought by Capt. Long (Bey) from the Soudan Expedition. It has a boldly curved steel blade and a wooden handle. The sheath and belt are of leather. The Nubian cimeter is, perhaps, even a little more curved than that shown from Soudan; but doubtless the weapons of a district vary, and are not confined rigidly to a certain curve, as in some countries where such things are defined in the "Regulations." The curve in each case is much greater than that of the *xóxix*, the east-

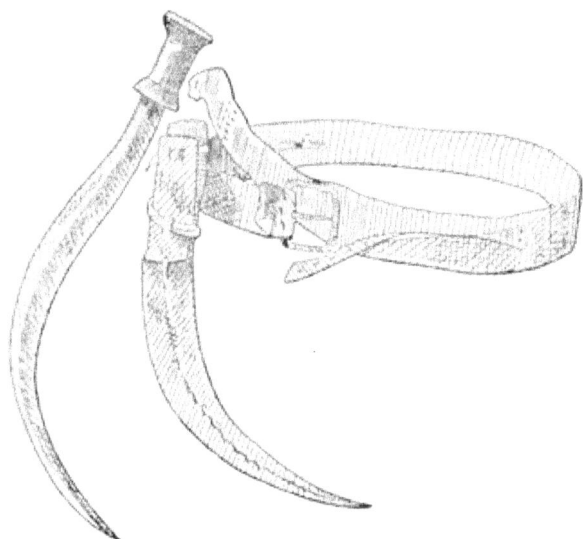

Fig. 87. — *Saber of Soudan, Africa.*

ern cimeter of classic times. The Apongos use a cimeter of similar shape, and with a handle shaped like a dice-box. The blade is 4 feet long. No other cimeter of Africa has so peculiar a bend as the *shotel* of the Abyssinians.[137] The blade is nearly straight for two feet, and then suddenly makes a turn of about sixty degrees. The edge is on the concave side, and it is intended that the point shall reach over the top of an enemy's shield. The blade is wider and heavier toward the point. It is of soft iron, has a rhinoceros-horn handle, and is swung on the right side.

Among the most curious weapons of the savage world are the hurling cimeters—if they may be so called—the *trumbashes* of the Niam-niams.[138] The term is from Sennaar, and refers generally to the missile weapons of the negroes. The *trumbash* of the Niam-niams (*kulbeda*) Fig. 26, consists ordinarily of several limbs of iron with pointed prongs and sharp edges. Somewhat similar implements are used by the tribes of the Tsad basin, and a weapon on the same principle is used by the Marghy and Musgoo. The Niam-niams carry them attached to the insides of their shields ready for duty, and hurl them with great rapidity, force, and accuracy. They are made by the skillful smiths of the Monbuttoo tribe of the Welle River. A hurling axe shaped like a sickle is also used by the troops of the scheik of Borneo. It is known as a *hunga-munga* and somewhat resembles the *trumbash* of the Niam-niams. The Tibboos, west of Nubia, use a missile sword, as do also the Fans of Western Africa. The Fan weapon is flat and pointed, and near the handle is a sharp projection.

137 Wood, vol. i, p. 718.   138 Schweinfurth's "Africa," vol. ii, p. 10.

The Malays and Dyaks have several swords, as they may be called, of peculiar character. Three of them are cutting weapons; the other is a thrust. The three former are *parangs*; the latter is the *kris*.

FIG. 88.—*The parang of the Malays.*

The *parang* [139] (Fig. 88) has a two-edged blade which is small but thick at the handle, and runs broader and thinner to near the point. It is elaborately ornamented with tufts of human hair and charms. The handle is frequently of deer bone neatly carved, but in the present instance is of wood bound with red leather and has a tuft of human hair at the hilt. The scabbard is of red wood, carved. A ratan-splitting knife [140] occupies a pocket in a small sheath attached to the scabbard of the *parang*. This attaching of a knife to the scabbard is also found in Scotland and Central Africa. The *parang-latok* is made of a square bar of ½-inch steel, which is gradually thinned and widened until it reaches a width of two inches near the point. It has a peculiar bend of 30° near the hilt. It is sword, machete, axe, all in one, being the ordinary weapon of the men and many of the women. It is kept in a wooden sheath made of two pieces of wood hollowed out and bound together with ratan. It is the executioner's weapon. The *parang-ihlang* is straight. Its blade has a curious shape, being ogee in cross-section. This shape seems to give it wonderful execution in cutting, but at the same time makes it dangerous to an inexpert swordsman, as the blade glances in a remarkable manner. The beheading sword of the piratical Illanos [141] has a somewhat similar curve. The holes in the Illanoon sword indicate the number of victims.

The most characteristic, however, of the Malay weapons is the *kris* [142] (Fig. 89), which is used in thrusting, as a Spaniard uses his knife. The armorers take as much pride in the making of the weapon as of old did the Toledo or Ferrara workmen. The blade is generally waving, and its grain is more marked than in any other weapon, as much so in fact as the Damascus gun-barrel, and for the same reason, as it is made of steel and iron strips laid together, twisted, doubled, and variously convoluted to give the kind of marking required. These are rendered more plain by etching the blade with lime juice, the acid corroding one metal

[139] Boyle's " Dyaks of Borneo," 114, 115;
Belcher's " Eastern Archipelago," ii. 133 and plate.
[140] Belcher's " Eastern Archipelago," vol. i, pp. 230, 231.   [141] *Ibid*, vol. i, p. 266.
[142] Raffles' " Java," 4to, i, p. 296 and plates ; Wallaces' " Malay."

more than the other, and hence leaving the surface grooved. The execution *kris* is also used as a thrust weapon, the *parang-latok* being used for beheading. The culprit or victim, as the case may be, sits in a chair, and his extended arms are held by two persons. The executioner stands behind and places the point of the kris just by the left collar bone, and strikes it downward,

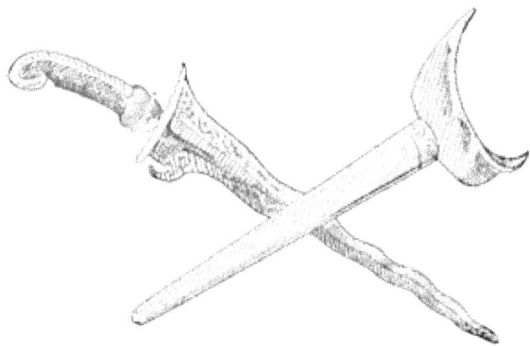

Fig. 89.—*Malay kris.*

piercing the heart. If he be fastidious he places a pledget of cotton wool around the point of the *kris* before thrusting it into the thorax, holds it there tightly, so as to wipe the weapon on its recovery, thrusts the wool into the gap, and thus avoids shedding a drop of blood.

"A most delicate monster."

It may be added that the kris is the most cherished possession of its owner, and may be worth $20, when his clothing would not command 25 cents. Some krises are heavily inlaid with gold. The sheath is of wood and comparatively plain. The size of the weapon is usually from 12 to 15 inches long, but larger ones are to be seen. Some authorities have told us that the handle is always bent at right angles to the blade. In the Javan collection of the Dutch colonies in the Main Building the handles were as represented in the figure.

Five swords of the Philippine Islands are represented in Fig. 90. They were in the Spanish Government Building. The resemblance to the Malaysian implements is very marked; *a* is evidently a *kris*; *b* is a *parang*; *c* is a *parang-ihlang*.

The Siamese sword [147] used from elephant back has a handle four feet long of heavy wood and a screw joint in the middle to make it more portable. The

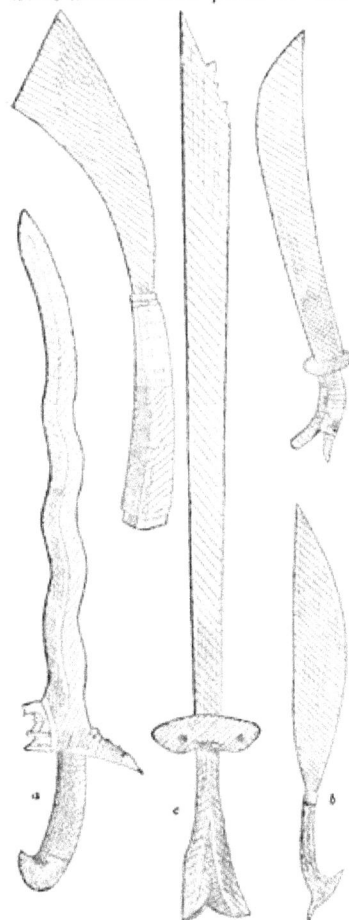

Fig. 90.—*Swords of the Philippines.*

[147] Ruschenberger's "Voyage Round the World," p. 295.

blade is one-edged, two feet long, and gently curved. The guard is a disk set with gems and the scabbard is enameled.

The Chinese use single swords, sometimes one in each hand; they also have two-handed swords.[144] The warrior armed with two makes them fly like the sails of a windmill, he leaping and dodging the while. The two-handed sword is of the same length and weight as the one exhibited from Norway. The Chinese also use a sword blade on the end of a pole. The practice of the Japanese of rank in carrying two swords is familiar from the many illustrations on the fans, which are so good and cheap. The swords are known as *ken* and *katten*. Some of the old Japanese swords have blood lines.[145]

The Norwegian two-handed sword of some centuries since was shown in the collection from that country in the Main Building. It has a whole length of 5½ feet and a hilt 15 inches in length. It has two hand-holds on the hilt and one above the hilt, probably to hold it when used as a pike.

IV.—SPEARS.

The spear is found among most savage nations and was the knightly weapon in Europe until the introduction of fire-arms. It, however, continued in use among the Poles, Russians, Turks, and Tartars, and was introduced into the armies of Prussia by Frederick the Great; the Austrians followed, calling the troops Uhlans, and lances are now found in most of the European cavalry forces. A number of lances were made for a cavalry regiment in the army of the Potomac, but the project was abandoned and the lances laid away in the arsenal in Washington.

Perhaps we may assume that the first spear was a sharpened stick or pole; such a one was shown in the collection from the Argentine Republic, a round pole a little larger than a hayfork handle, of dark wood and 10 feet long. The point was a simple taper without any attempt at hastate form.

FIG. 91.—*Norwegian two-handed sword.*

A common spear of Borneo and the Philippines is a sharpened bamboo, such as shown at *a b*, Fig. 92. In one case the shaft is of bamboo, and in the other a bamboo head is slipped upon a cocoa-wood shaft. The end is so sharpened that the hard silicious skin of the bamboo forms the edge and makes a very efficient cutting and piercing weapon. The spears *c d* are of cocoa wood. The head of *c* has an ornament resembling

[144] Wood, vol. ii, p. 314.

[145] Siebold's "Nippon," ii, plates 3, 5 *bis*, 12.

six diminishing ears of corn with a round finial point. Similarly ornamented spear heads are made in Fiji. The other (*d*) has six gradually
decreasing sets of barbs
crowned by a finial. Other
spears from the Philippines
had shark's teeth tacked to
ridges on the head, and some
had metallic heads. They will
be shown presently.

Jagor mentions that the
spear (*pica*) of the Philippines
is of caryota wood 2.27ᵐ long;
the head of bamboo, carved
wood, or iron (purchased).[116]

The large spear of the Sandwich Islands[117] is 12 or 15 feet
long and is not barbed, but
the hurling spear is 6 or 8 feet
long, of hard wood, and tapers
toward the butt, to throw the
center of gravity forward of
the mid-length and enable it
to fly straight.

The Fijians,[118] who excel in
ingenuity, have several kinds
of spears. The fishing spear
has three or four points set
in separately. Each point has
a round, square, or semicircu-
lar section, is dovetailed into
the shaft and lashed thereto
with *sinnet*. The war spear
has a carved head, and barbs,
either cut in the wood, or
made of the tail of the sting-
ray and set in separately;
these brittle barbs come off
in the wound and insure cruel
suffering and generally death.
One Fijian spear is made of
a wood which bursts when
moist, so that it is with difficulty extracted. The different islands, such as the Tonga,
Herveys, Fiji, and the New Hebrides have distinguishable varieties of
spears.

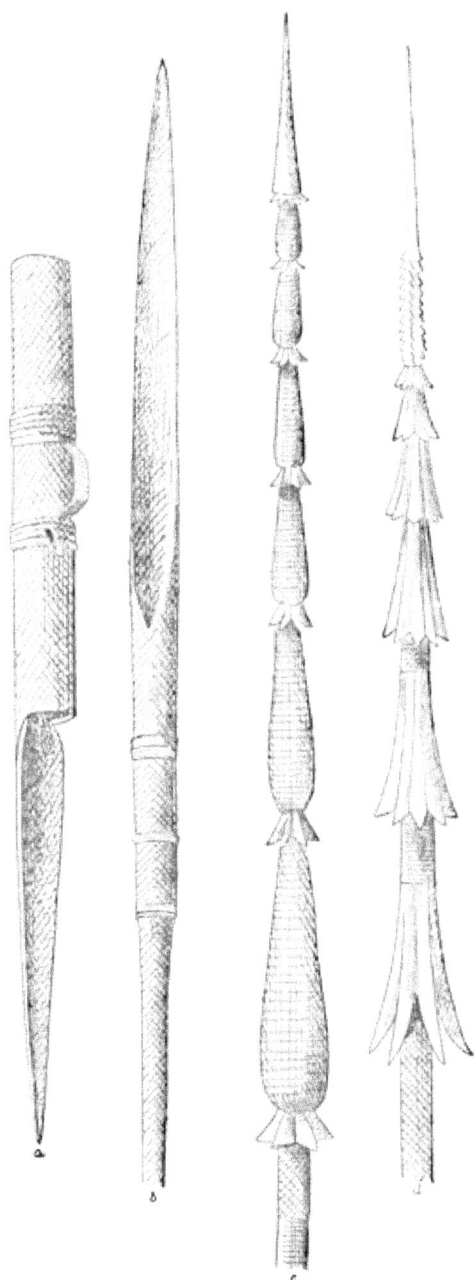

FIG. 92.—*Spears of the Philippines.*

[116] "Philippines," p. 240. [117] Wood, vol. ii, p. 434. [118] Williams "Fiji," pp. 44-5.

The Australian spears are of various qualities and shapes: a sharpened stick (*nandum*) with notches for barbs;[149] a spear with a separate head of hard *miall* wood deeply cut with barbs, and fastened to a reed (*phragmites communis*) shaft;[150] one with a basalt or quartzite head lashed to the shaft with sinews from the tail of the kangaroo,[151] with long projecting barbs on each side, curiously formed from hard wood,[152] a single bone lashed to the head and projecting laterally and backwardly from the point so as to form a barb; the *mongile*, a head armed with sharp basalt or quartzite flakes set with *pid-jer-ong* gum;[153] one with a head piece of bone which is lashed to the shaft so that its respective ends form point and barb;[154] lastly, leisters with from two to four barbed points,[155] and from 6 to 15 feet long.

The flower stalk of the grass-tree furnishes the spear-shaft, which is 9 or 10 feet long. Fig. 93 shows two South Australian spears, one with a double set of inserted barbs made of obsidian or quartz, and a kangaroo spear with a wooden head 30 inches long, and a single row of barbs; the shaft is 8 feet long. Fig. 94 shows two fish-spears, one with two prongs and the other with three. The prongs of hard and tough gum-tree wood are tapered towards each end, pointed, and barbed; their butt-ends are then inserted in notches on the end of the shaft and held in position by black-boy gum, while the prongs are spread apart by wedges driven between them. The prongs are then lashed with sinews. The Australian has a blade on the end of his spear to act as a paddle as he stands in his dug-out canoe and watches the water or quietly moves from place to place. The night is the favorite time for fish-spearing, a fire being made on a bed of wet sand

Fig. 93.—*Australian wooden spears.*

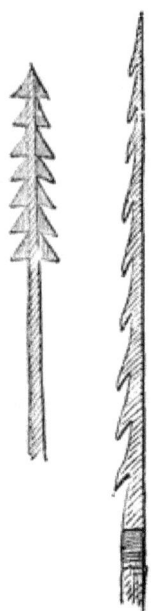

Fig. 94.—*Australian wooden fishing-spears (leisters.)*

and stones in the bottom of the canoe. The natives also carry torches of inflammable bark; this mode of fishing is common in North America and in Scotland, called "burning the water" in the former, and "leistering" in the latter.

[149] R. Brough Smith, "Aborigines of Victoria," vol. i, p. 304, Fig. 71–74.

[150] *Ibid.*, vol. i, p. 305, Figs. 75, 76.

[151] *Ibid.*, vol. i, p. 302, Fig. 85.

[152] *Ibid.*, vol. i, Figs. pp. 69, 70, and i, 302, Fig. 84.

[153] *Ibid.*, vol. i, p. 304, Fig. 68, and i, 336, Fig. 141.

[154] *Ibid.*, vol. i, p. 306, Fig. 77, 78.

[155] *Ibid.*, vol. i, p. 306, Figs. 79, 80, p. 337, Fig. 144 *et al.* See also Pl. iv, and pp. 33–5 Nilson's "Stone Age."

The large spear of the Australian, not to be thrown but used as a pike, is as much as 13 feet in length, the head of hard wood, the shaft of lighter wood, and as large as the wrist. The Australians also use a forked spear, *bobo*, to secure eels and snakes alive.[156] The turtle harpoon, like the hippopotamus harpoon of Africa, has a head detachable from the shaft. To the head is attached a rope, on the other end of which is a buoy. The harpoon for the dugong has a bone head 4 inches long and covered with barbs. It becomes detached from the shaft after striking; the cord attached to the spear-head has no float, but is secured on board the canoe. The simplest form of fish spear is a long sharp stick used in gigging fish in water-holes.[157]

The spears in the New Zealand department were all of wood. Some were simply pointed poles of hard wood; others had carved heads with pyramidal points. The spear is not a favorite weapon of the Maoris; in fact is said to have been laid aside. The heads of the spears are understood to be a conventional representation of the human tongue thrust out. That shown in Fig. 95 is destitute of ornament; Fig. 96, called by the natives *taiaha kura*, has suspended tufts of dyed hair.

The styles of ornamentation peculiar to New Zealand, New Guinea, and Fiji are referred to by R. Brough Smith.[158]

The harpoon of the Andaman Islander[159] is shot from a bow, and has a detachable head with a connected cord, which is held by the archer.

The spears already considered are made of wood, although the use of the tail of the sting-ray by the Fijians and of bone and obsidian by the Australians have been incidentally mentioned. Materials in great variety have been used for the heads or barbs of spears.

Stone spear-heads were shown in the South Australian department. They were obtained from the northern part of the island near Melville's Island. They are genuine specimens of the stone age, which does not represent a specific time but a grade of civilization. Consideration must also be had to the absence of metals in some localities. The stone spear-heads are chipped to shape and lashed to reed shafts with sinews, or with fiber obtained from roots. The reeds are 6 feet long and the heads from 4 to 6 inches.

The spears of the Solomon Islanders are tipped with sharp flints; those of the Admiralty Islanders are of obsidian lashed to the shaft and coated

FIG. 95.—*Maori wooden spear.*

FIG. 96.—*Maori spear taiaha kura.*

[156] Aborigines of Victoria, vol. i, p. 307, Fig. 82.   [157] *Ibid.*, vol. i, p. 307, Fig. 81.
[158] *Ibid.*, vol. i, pp. 296, 297.   [159] Mouat "Andaman," p. 326.

with gum. The Mexican spears were pointed with obsidian. The obsidian spear-heads of the Papuans excited the surprise of Schouten, an early navigator in those seas; he remarks that they had "long staves with very long, sharp things at the ends thereof, which, as we thought, were finnes of black fishes."[160] The aborigines of the Canaries, a race of African origin, when first discovered, used hatchets, knives, lancets, and spear-heads of obsidian, and axes of green jasper.

The lances found in the upper strata during the excavations at Hissarlik [161] were of a very hard black or green stone. The spear of the Northern American Indian was formerly of stone or flint, but is now of steel.[162]

We may refer in a single group to those spears which are tipped with animal material, bone, horn, shell, shark's teeth, claws of beasts and birds (such as of the kangaroo, cassowary, or emu), and the tail of the sting-ray. In the times of Herodotus and Strabo, African spears were headed with the sharpened horns of antelopes,[163] and the practice still obtains.[164] The Canary Islanders, when discovered, in the fourteenth century, had spears and digging-sticks tipped with horns.[165] Fig. 98 shows two Kajäk

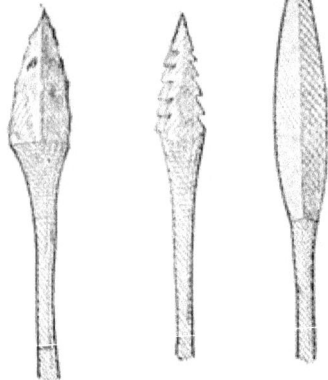

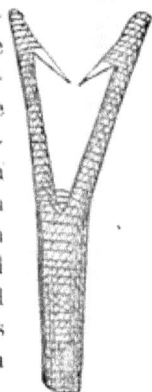

FIG. 97.—Stone spear-heads, South Australia.

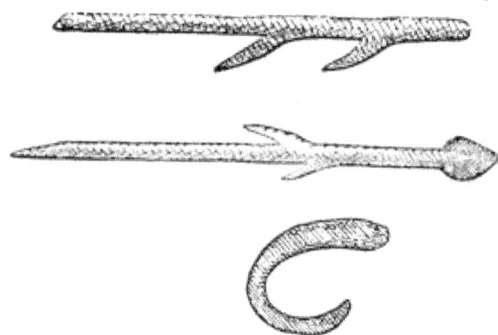

FIG. 98.—Bone spear-heads and hook, Greenland.

FIG. 99.—Wooden fish-spear. Makah of British Columbia.

spear-heads and a hook of bone, exhibited in the Greenland section of the Danish department. The upper one is cut down so as to leave barbs. The next beneath it has an iron tip riveted to the bone. The lower example is a bone hook about 2 inches across. Barbed harpoons of bone, from a Scanian bog, Sweden, from a cave in Perigord, and from Terra del Fuego, are shown in Nilson's "Stone Age."[166]

[160] Purchas, vol. i, p. 95.
[161] "Schliemann's Troy, &c.," p. 79.
[162] Dr. Abbott in Smithsonian Report, 1875, pp. 269, 274.
[163] Herod., vii, 69-71. Strabo, xvi, 4, 9, 11.
[164] Andersson, p. 15.
[165] Tylor, p. 222, and note passim.
[166] Plate iv, Figs. 69, 70, 72.

Fig. 99 is a fish-spear head of wood with incurved points or barbs of bone; the binding is of cherry bark. These hooks are used by the Makahs and other Northwestern Indians.

Fig. 100 is a fish-spear of the Chookchees (*Tschucklochies*) of Northeast Siberia. It has a long stout shaft of pine wood, only one-half the length of which is shown. The head consists of two baleen prongs, on the ends of which are lashed two incurved points of ivory, forming barbs. The same style of fish-spear is used by the Youcon Indians of the Mackenzie River country.[167] The Fuegan fishing-spear is 10 feet long and has an octagonal shaft with a bone head 7 inches in length, with a single barb.

The National Museum in the Government Building had specimens of whale and seal lances from Siberia, Alaska, and Greenland.

Fig. 101 is a seal-spear from the Chookchees of Northeast Siberia. It has a long spliced pine-wood handle and movable point of bone with a metallic tip.

Harpoons with movable[168] and immovable points[169] are shown in Sven Nilson's "Stone Age," edited by Sir John Lubbock.

Fig. 102 is a whaling-lance from the Ponook Eskimo of Alaska. It is pointed with a portion of a marrow-bone cut off obliquely so as to afford a long cutting-edge. The butt-end has a flattened piece to fit the throwing-board, which will be shown presently. The piece on the side is a spur or button to prevent the spear penetrating the whale too far. The Ostiaks, Chookchees, and Keriaks secure the same end

Fig. 100.—*Chookchee fish-spear, Siberia.*

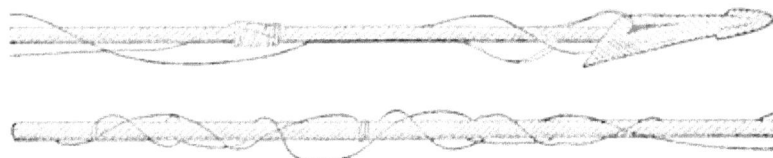

Fig. 101.—*Seal-spear of the Chookchees, Northeast Siberia.*

by binding the shaft with raw sea-lion hide, which, drying, forms an im-

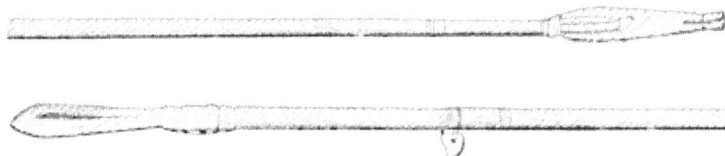

Fig. 102.—*Whaling-lance of Alaska Eskimo.*

movable ridge. Fig. 103 is a whaling-lance of the Greenland Eskimo.

[167] Smithsonian Report for 1866, p. 324.
[168] "Stone Age," Plate iii, Figs. 52, 53 (for bladder spears).
[169] *Ibid.* Plate iii, 41, 50, 51; Plate iv, 69, 72 (bone tips and bone tipped with stone).

It has an iron snow-rest at the end of the wooden stock; the shaft is of iron and has a walrus-ivory point, which comes free of the shaft when the whale is struck. The shaft is dragged by the whale, and a float may be secured to the end of the thong. The thongs for the Eskimo harpoons are made from the skins of a large species of seal. Incisions six inches apart are made completely around the body and the rings of hide removed like so many hoops. These are then cut spirally into thongs of a length equal to the circumference of the body at the part multiplied by the number of times the width of the thongs goes into 6 inches. Fig. 104 is another whaling-lance of the Greenland Eskimo. It has a long bone rod for the attachment of the movable head which comes entirely free of the shaft, but is held by the thong. The shaft has a snow-rest at the butt.

The Makah Indians of the Northwest Coast use a lance and seal-skin buoy in capturing the great bow-head whales of the Pacific. Fig. 105 shows the buoy, rope, and lance-head. The head is placed on the end of a long forked pole and comes off the shaft after the whale is struck. The buoy is made of a seal-skin stripped off entire, sown up at the ends, and inflated. The lance-head is of shell with walrus-ivory barbs and point secured with sinews and pitch. The rope is of spruce root roasted in the ashes, pounded, frayed, and twisted. Fig. 106 shows the seal and fish-spear of the Eskimo of Kodiak, Alaska. It has a long slender ornamented shaft and movable barbed point. The shaft has a bladder float and an ivory knob to limit the penetration of the spear.

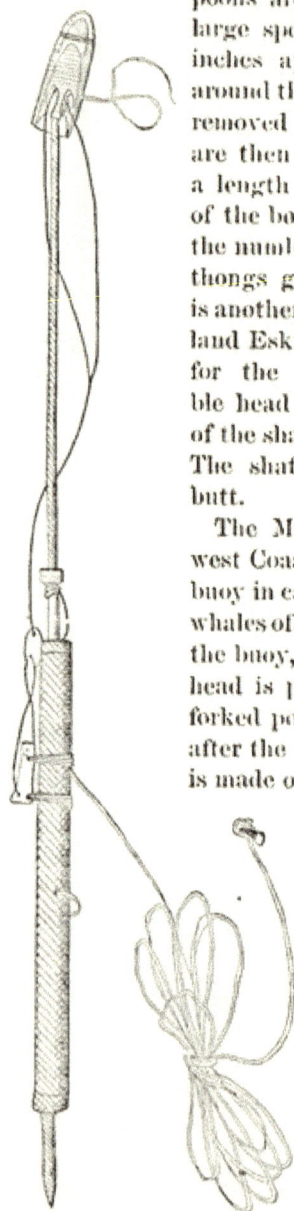

Fig. 103.—*Whaling-lance, Greenland.*

Fig. 104.—*Whaling-lance of Greenland Eskimo.*

The bird spear of the Greenland Eskimo has, besides its main point, several supplementary points at some distance from the end of the spear. It has an inflated bladder to prevent its sinking in the water.

A number of different Polynesian weapons are made with shark's teeth lashed to wooden clubs or lances. Fig. 107 is a spear-

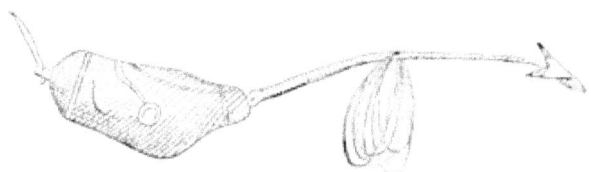

FIG. 105.—*Lance head and seal buoy, British Columbia.*

head exhibited in the Philippine Islands section of the Spanish department. The Kingsmill and Marquesas Islanders also arm the edges of their spears with sharks' teeth, binding them to the shaft with sinnet, the plaited fiber (*coir*) of the cocoa-nut. One from the Kingsmill Islands has over 200 teeth in a row, the shaft being of light wood and 15 feet long. A spear from the Philippines had 72 teeth in a row. A saw is made on the same principle by the Australians; flakes of obsidian or quartz, about the size of a quarter-dollar, are inserted in a grooved stick of gum-tree wood and fastened by gum from the grass-tree, commonly known as "black-

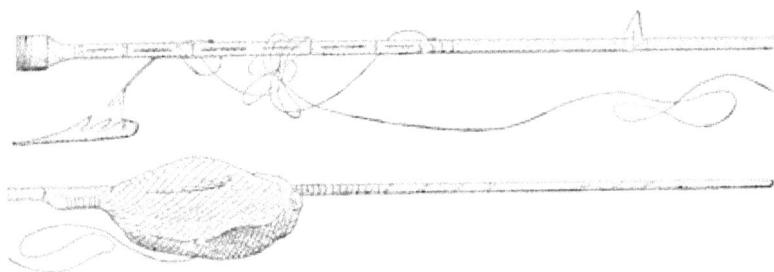

FIG. 106.—*Seal and fish spear, Kodiak Eskimo, Alaska.*

boy" gum."[170] Javelins of bone or wood with longitudinal grooves, in which are inserted flint flakes, are shown by Nilson.[171]

The spear of the Tonga Islands is barbed with the tail bone of the sting-ray; the same bone is used on the prongs of the Tahitian trident. The barbs are not fastened, but are slipped into sockets just tight enough to hold them until they are thrust into the body, when they become detached and, from their barbed character, work deeper and deeper into the wound.

We have considered wooden spears, and those with stone and bone heads, and incidentally some other materials. We now come to metal, the material of all the best, and which, once adopted, is not again laid aside.

Spear-heads of copper were shown among the Indian implements from Wisconsin. Copper preceded iron, being found native and malleable. Copper and bronze implements are among the articles recovered from the Egyptian tombs, the tumuli of Assyria, and the excavations of Hissarlik.[172] The spears of the Peruvians[173] were tipped with copper or bone, and those of the Inca lords mounted with gold and silver.

The Philippine Islands were represented in the Spanish Government building, and had a sheaf of spears, among which were the iron weapons, Fig. 108. One of these has a sword-blade, and a number of ferrules to prevent the tang from splitting the shaft. Another spear has two barbs, and a third one has a lanceolate head. The trident, Fig. 110, was also shown in the same collection. The *mora*, or cross-bar, to limit the penetration of the spears, shown in the Roman *venabulum* or hog spear, does not seem to be in common use in the Orient. The Japanese have as many as 14 kinds of spears,[174] perhaps more.

Fig. 109 is a three-pointed spear from Timor, shown in the collection from the Portuguese colonies. It has three simple points, the outer ones being on the ends of a cross-bar slipped over the middle prong and bent forward. The Philippine trident, Fig. 110, is used for fishing, but the Illanoon pirates[175] use a bifurcated spear with retreating barbs to catch men by the neck. The three-pointed spear is found in many widely separated parts of the world, and is mentioned in the history of the Saracen conquests, particularly in one of the feats of Ali. Fig. 111 shows three spears of the Island of Timor. They show the same tendency as to shape as the halberds and lances of the middle

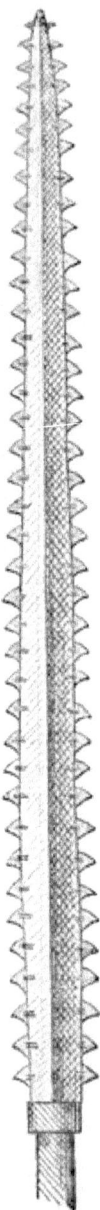

FIG. 107.— *Shark's-tooth spear of the Philippines.*

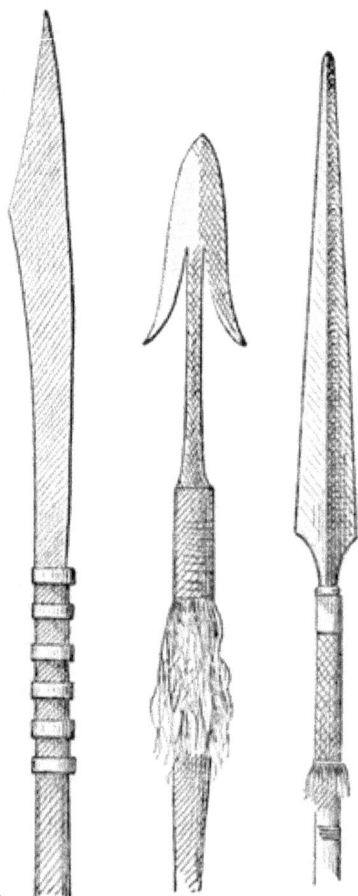

FIG. 108.— *Iron spear-heads of the Philippines.*

[172] "Troy and its Remains," p. 330.   [173] "Conquest of Peru," vol. i, p. 73.
[174] Siebold's "Nippon," vol. ii, pl. 6.   [175] Belcher's "Eastern Archipelago," vol. i, p. 252.

ages. The weapons of Timor and of the Philippines are very similar, as might have been anticipated.

The African spears show a great variety. Over the large portion of the continent iron is either plentiful or readily accessible by means of the native traders. The metallurgic process is a direct one from the ore and the product is a steel. Weights, shapes, and sizes of the weapons differ greatly. The Bongos of the Upper Nile[176] are skillful blacksmiths and make excellent lances, especially considering the crude

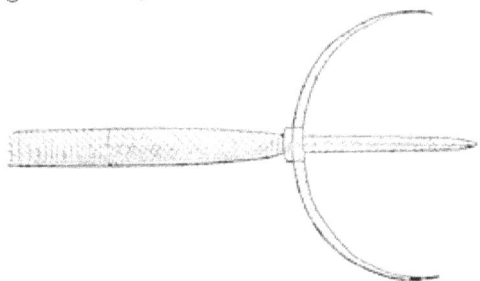

Fig. 109.—*Trident of Timor.*

character of their tools. The spears of the Niam-niams and Monbuttoos[177] are of a hastate shape, and their weapons all have blood grooves, which dis-

Fig. 110.—*Trident of the Philippines.*

tinguishes them from the weapons of the Bongo and Mittoo. The Man-ganji spear[177] is sometimes made with a paddle or dibble at the end of the handle, and is weighted with iron rings.

The spear of the Kanemboo infantry soldier of Borneo is 7 feet in length, and armed below the head with a number of hook-shaped barbs. The Abyssinian spear is seven feet long and has four grooved sides. It is used either as a pike or a javelin. The natives have also a way of throwing it at close quarters by letting the shaft pass through the hand and catching the butt-end. The bark of a young tree being removed, the wood is seasoned by fire, greased, then hung in the sun to obtain the desired color.

The hippopotamus spear of the Zambesi[178] is a beam four or five feet long armed with a spear-head or hard-wood spike covered with poison. The spear is suspended from a forked pole by a cord, which, coming down close

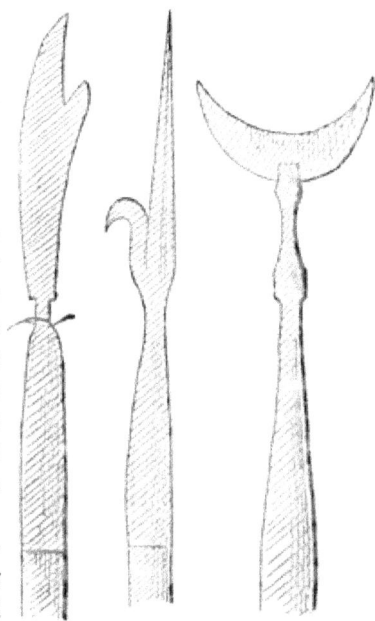

Fig. 111.—*Spears of Timor.*

[176] Schweinfurth's "Africa," vol. i, p. 280.

[177] Ibid., vol. ii, p. 27.

[178] Livingstone's "Zambesi," p. 532.

[179] Livingstone's Zambesi, p. 107; Baker's Ismailia, Pl. opp., p. 135.

to the path frequented by the animals, is held by a catch and is set free when the animal treads upon it. The Banyai of the Zambesi have a hippopotamus spear with a wooden shaft, iron head, and weighted with stones; like the former, it is suspended over the track of the animals. The Fans of the Gaboon have a similar contrivance. The Dôr tribe prepares a similar spear, but the hunter climbs a tree and drops it upon an elephant passing beneath. The elephant spear of Unyoro is similar.

The hippopotamus harpoon of the Zambesi[150] has an iron head inserted in the end of a long pole of light wood. The head has a stout barb and becomes detached from the shaft ; the rope attached to the head unreels from the shaft, and when it has all run out the shaft acts as a float to indicate the locality of the animal. An inflated bladder is sometimes used as a float. The rope is made from the bark of the *milola*, an umbrageous hibiscus. The Hamram Arabs use a float of *ambatch*, an extremely light wood. The Makobahs of Lake Ngami[151] attach the rope to the head by a large bunch of loose strands, which cannot be cut clean off by the teeth of the animal. A rope of palm leaf is attached to the shaft, and is coiled up in the boat.

The turtle-spear of the Central American Indians is a heavy palm-wood staff with a notched iron peg at the end, and twenty fathoms of silk-grass line attached.

The *assegai*, the hurling spear or javelin of the Kafirs, was shown in the Cape of Good Hope collection. It is a very formidable weapon in

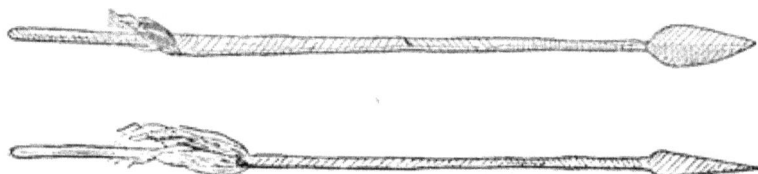

FIG. 112.—*Kafir assegais.*

the hands of this athletic and untamed people. The people of "the Cape" say that the Kafirs are the remains of the lost "ten tribes of Israel," and have fought their way all down through Africa. Their assegais are made from native iron, have wooden shafts, and are decorated with tufts of cow hair. The blade has various symmetrical lanceolate shapes. A ridge passes along the center of the blade, which is concave on one side, convex on the other. This shape is intended to give rotation to the weapon. The head of the assegai is about the size of the blade of a table-knife, and has a tang which is inserted by burning it while red-hot into a shaft of assegai wood (*Curtisia faginea*), which resembles mahogany. The two parts are secured by lashings of raw hide, which contracts in drying and holds all firmly. The *assegai* is the main weapon of the Kafir, and with it he kills his cattle, skins them, and cuts them up; with it he also carves his clubs, spoons, dishes, pillows, and milk-

[150] Livingstone's Zambesi, p. 44.　　　[151] Wood, vol. i, p. 379.

pots, and shaves his head—or rather that of his friend. His other weapon is a club; he does not use the bow and arrow.

The Bechuana *assegais*[132] have cruel barbs on their shafts, being originally forged square and the barbs made by cutting and raising the corners. . The *assegai* of the Damaras has a broad, leaf-shaped, soft-iron blade a foot in length; it has a strong handle, on which is a flowing ox-tail.

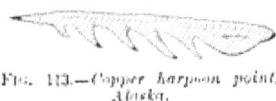

FIG. 113.—*Copper harpoon point, Alaska.*

The spear of the Gran Chaco Indian of La Plata is 15 feet long; it is his principal war weapon, and is also used as a vaulting-pole in mounting his horse. The Fuegain throwing-spear is shorter and has a row of barbs down one side.

The harpoon-point of native copper, with unilateral barbs, is shown in Fig. 113. It is from the Atnaes of Copper River, Alaska. The harpoon used by the Ahts of Vancouver's Island in whale-fishing has a yew handle ten feet long, on the end of which is a detachable iron barbed blade; it has a line of deer sinews connecting with the main cord of cedar-bark twine laid up into a rope and having a number of inflated seal skins attached.

The fish-spear of the Frobisher Bay Eskimo, Fig. 114, has a point of iron, and incurved barbs made from sharpened nails set in flexible bone prongs, which are lashed to the short pine-wood handle. Fig. 115 is the salmon spear of the Passamaquoddy Indians. It has a long stout shaft, wooden prongs, and iron point.

Norway sent some relics of the past, the halberds and lances, Fig. 116.

Throwing-sticks are used in many parts of the world to increase the power of flight of the spear by extending the radius of the arm in throwing. The throw-stick of the Australians,

FIG. 114.—*Fishspear, Frobisher Bay Eskimo.*

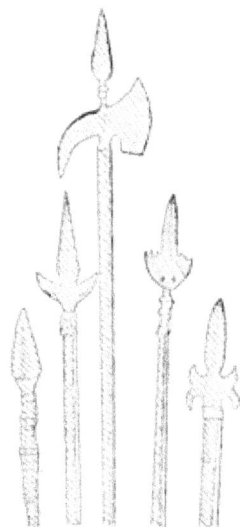

FIG. 116.—*Norwegian halberds.*

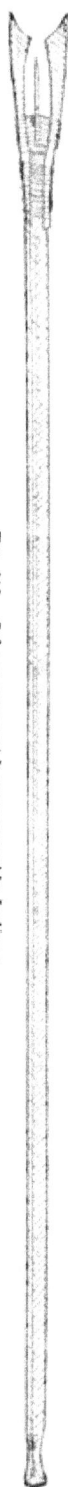

FIG. 115.—*Salmon spear of Passamaquoddy Indians.*

called by them *Wummerah*[182] *midlah*, *meera*, *kur-wuk*, is a stick[184] about three feet long. The spear lies along the arm and the stick, its rear end being against the prong on the outer end of the latter. The butt of the spear has a socket for the tooth on the end of the stick. This is sometimes a tooth of a kangaroo; in other cases of bone or of wood. The form of the *wummerah* varies in different parts of the island, being sometimes a mere stick with a swelled hand-hold at one end and the prong at the other. Other specimens show that boards, leaf-shaped or tapering. It is of hard and elastic wood, and heavy enough to be used as a club at close quarters. The spear is quivered like the Kafir assegai in throwing, and undulates like a thin black snake in its passage through the air. It is also thrown underhand, skimming and ricocheting on the ground. Figs. 117 and 118 are throwing-sticks of South Australia and Victoria, shown in the Main Building.

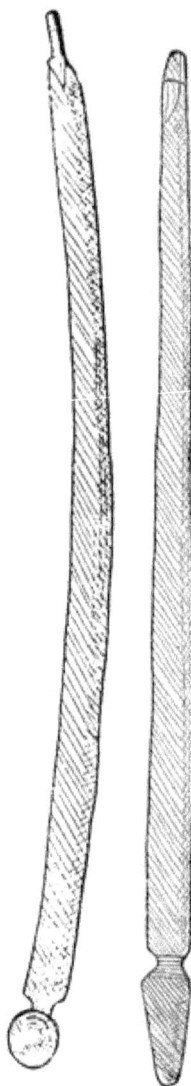

Fig. 119 shows the way of using it. The plan reminds one of the Spanish method of knife-throwing, in which the fore-arm and hand are used as the projector, the knife lying in the hand, which is extended palm upward.

Although the plan of bending the spears in throwing does not appear to be universal in Australia, it is sometimes adopted to increase the force of the projection. The Pelew Islanders use a throwing-stick about two feet long to hold the butt of the spear, which, in throwing, is bent by the left hand until it is nearly double. The spear is released by the left hand simultaneously with the sweeping motion of the right hand and arm. The Purupurus of the Amazon,[185] unlike all the other tribes of the region, have neither blow-gun nor bow, but project their arrows by means of a throwing-stick (*pulheta*). Like the Australian and American implements it has a projection at the end to hold the

FIG. 117.—*Spear-throwing sticks, South Australia.*

FIG. 118.—*Throwing-stick of Victoria, Australia.*

[1] Backhouse's "Australia," p. 433.

[2] R. Brough Smith. "Aborigines of Victoria," vol. i, pp. 308, 309, Figs. 88–93, and p. 338, Figs. 146, 147.

[3] Wallace's "Amazon," p. 514.

butt of the arrow. The middle of the arrow and the handle of the *pal-heta* are held in the right hand, and the arrow is projected as from a sling. The natives are very skillful with it.

The throwing-boards used by the Northwestern Eskimo and Indians are shown in Fig. 120. They resemble the spear-casters (*xuiatla-tli*) used by the Aztecs at the time of the Span-ish conquest. On the

FIG. 119.—*Australian throwing-stick.*

mural monuments of Mexico the gods are generally represented as using the stick to throw the javelin. The Mexican stick most resembles the upper one in Fig. 118. Some other Eskimo throwing-sticks have pro-jections against which the butt of the spear is placed; and others (see the lower in the figure) have holes for the tail end of the spear.

The Romans used the *amentum* (*cf. habena*), a thong fastened at the center of gravity of the javelin to hurl the weapon. It is mentioned by Livy and Ovid. By giving the thong a few turns around the shaft a ro-tary motion could be imparted to the javelin in throwing. The *ansa* of the *ansa-tahasta* was a sem-icircular strap-handle to a spear, like the bow on a sword-hilt. The *aclis* of the ancient

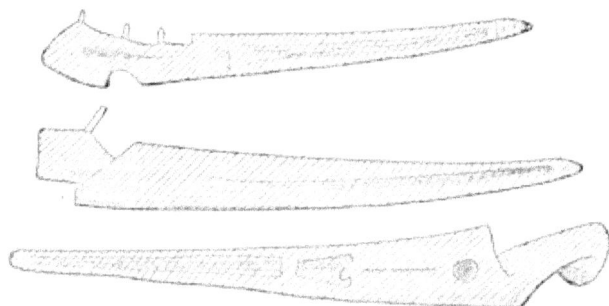

FIG. 120.—*Throwing-boards of Northwestern Eskimo.*

Osci was a massive spear like a harpoon, with an attached line for recov-ering it.

The natives of New Caledonia have a javelin 15 feet long, which is discharged by a plaited cord (*ounep*) attached a little behind the middle of the spear. This *ounep* (otherwise called *sipp*), answering to the *amen-tum* of the ancients, but superior thereto, is a plaited cord made of com-bined coir fiber and fish-skin; it has a knot at one end and is worked into a loop at the other. It is wound around the spear-shaft so as to give it a rotary motion in flying.[196] When a spear is to be thrown the forefinger of the right hand is put into the loop, and the man balancing the weapon to find the middle takes a sailor's half-hitch at a point behind the center of gravity. Throwing the spear he looses his grasp at once, projecting the weapon by the cord, which becomes detached as soon as the back-ward pull on it occurs, leaving the cord in the hand of the thrower. The ancient *amentum* was attached to the spear.

---

[196] Nilson, "Stone Age," p. 174.

V.—SHIELDS.

Shields were in force, in Philadelphia, from Africa, Asia, Malaysia, and Australia. They were of grass, ratan, hide, wood, and other materials. Some were so large as to cover the person; others were smaller and intended to be moved to intercept a weapon; others still were long and narrow, used in parrying spear-thrusts.

Beginning with the South of Africa, the first we find is the Zulu shield in the department of the Cape of Good Hope. It is of ox-hide and of a long elliptical shape. The color denotes service. Black shields are for boys; white, with mottlings, for warriors. The prevalence of color or peculiar markings denotes the regiment to which the warrior belongs. The shield is strengthened by a vertical stake at the rear, which forms a handle, and projects below and above, where it forms a rest and an ornament, respectively. A strip of black hide is passed in and out of a double row of slits, one row on each side of the stick, showing on the front of the shield like oblong markings on a white ground. Standing on its end the shield comes up to the warrior's eyes, the stick to the crown of his head. The shields are the property of the chief, and are apportioned to the deserving. The shapes of the shields vary among the different tribes of what may be called the Kafir race. Some of the shields have depressions in the sides as if a piece had been cut out, resembling the *ancile* or sacred shield of Numa, which was supposed to have fallen from Heaven. In some instances the depressions in the sides are so great as to make them hour-glass shaped. The Basuto Kafirs[17] have a curious shield, resembling a body with two wings. The Bechuana have a shield smaller than the Zulus and cut from the thickest part of an ox-hide. The Barolongs and Batlapis have a rectangular shield, edged at top and bottom with two rounded wings.

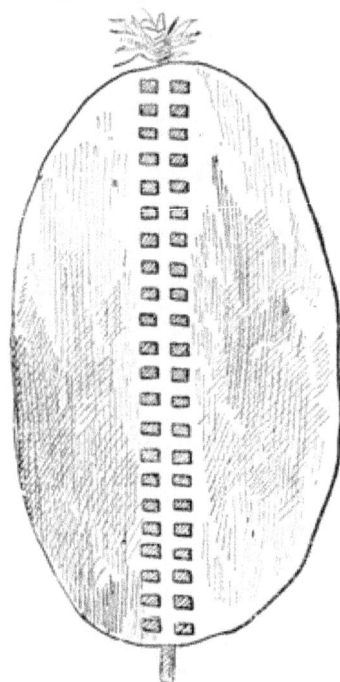

Fig. 121.—*Zulu shield of ox-hide.*

Passing northward and reaching the latitude of Portuguese occupation, we find the mat shield of Angola, Fig. 122, made of a species of grass growing commonly in many parts of Africa. The same style of manufacture is shown almost all along the Western Coast—the baskets and mats of the Gold Coast, for instance. The grass is made into long

[17] Casalis' "Basutos," pp. 63, 135, 136; Livingstone's "Zambesi," Pl. opp. p. 40.

rolls, which are laid spirally, being interlaced by ratan strips which proceed from the center radially. The view shows the back of the shield with the two sticks which form the handle. The shields of Londa-land, in Equatorial Africa, on the West Coast, are made of reeds plaited together. The shape is oblong-square, 5 feet by 2. The Apono shields are circular and of basket-work. The shield of the Fans of the Gaboon [16] is a piece of hide 3 feet long and 2½ feet wide from the skin of the elephant's shoulder. This resists all the native weapons: axes, spears, arrows, or even bullets in a glancing direction.

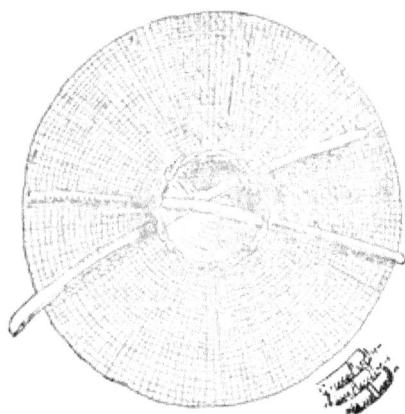

FIG. 122.—Mat shield of Angola.

The Egyptian collection showed a number of shields from Central Africa, trophies brought north by Long Bey from his expedition beyond Khartoom. Fig. 123 is a leathern conical shield with a handle of the same. It is 2 feet in diameter; altitude of cone, 6 inches. It is made of ox hide and has a strong leathern binding. It is ornamented to represent basket-work. Another shield exhibited was of giraffe hide and 1 foot in diameter. The Roman *clipeus* was a round buckler of several folds of ox hide covered with plates of metal and sometimes on a wicker-work foundation. Fig. 123 shows the strap, answering to the Roman *balteus*, by which the shield was suspended from the shoulder.

The Dinkas of the Upper Nile [17] use an ox-hide shield like the Kafirs. It is cut in oval form and crossed by a stick secured by being passed through holes cut in the thick leather.

Allied to the shield is an instrument used among the Dinkas and Niam-niams for parrying clubs and lances, rather than actually covering the body. One Dinka instrument looks so much like a bow that it has been mistaken for one; this is called *dang*. The other is a neatly carved piece of wood about a yard long and with a hollow at the mid-length for the hand-grasp. A similar parrying shield

FIG. 123.—Leathern shield of Uganda, Africa.

[16] Wood, vol. i, p. 596.   [17] Schweinfurth's "Africa," vol. i, p. 155.

is found in Australia (see *infra*, Fig. 134). The Niam-niams use a spindle shaped wooden implement 4 inches broad in the middle and tapering to a point at each end. It is carried in the left hand, a handle being scooped out of the center, and is used in parrying lances and spears by means of a dexterous twist.

The wooden shield of Uganda is shown in Fig. 124. The wood is soft, ornamented with ratan and bound with leather. It is 2 feet 10 inches long, 2 feet wide, and half an inch thick. The wood projects in the center to form a boss; the handle is of ratan. A basket-work shield from Uganda, also from the Long Bey collection, is shown in Fig. 125. It is made of cane strips sewed together with ratan over ribs of split wood. It is 3 feet 8 inches long by 15 inches wide. The edge is bound with raw-hide, and in the center is a block 18 by 6 inches with a handle cut in it. It is tied to the shield with ratan,

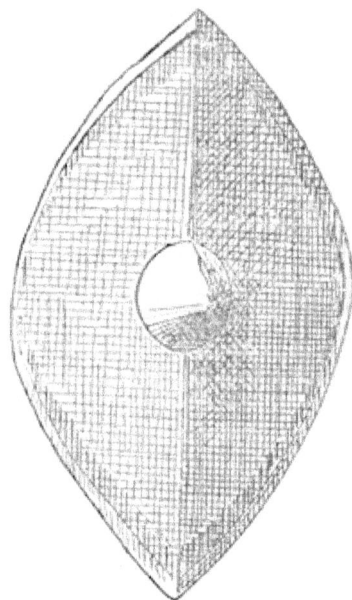

FIG. 124.—*Wooden shield, Central Africa.*

FIG. 125.—*Basket-work shield, Uganda, Africa.*

and serves to strengthen the shield as well as afford a hold for the hand.

The shield of the Niam-niams[120] is plaited from the Spanish reed, and is of a long oval form covering two-thirds of the body. It is plaited in pretty patterns of black and white in crosses and is lined with leopard skin. Inside of the shield the native carries the *trumbash*, a peculiar missile weapon with blades and three projecting points. See *supra*.

The Monbuttoos who inhabit the territory south of the Niam-niams of the extreme Upper Nile waters have a wooden shield of rectangular

[120] Schweinfurth's "Africa," vol. i, p. 441; vol. ii, pp. 9–11.

shape, somewhat like, but flatter than, the Roman *scutum*.[191]   The shield is 4 feet by 2½ feet, half an inch thick, and is hewn out of the solid block. It has a ridge-like protuberance across the middle and is stiffened and ornamented with transverse plates of copper and *rotang* twist.   The shields are usually decorated with tails of the guinea-hog (*Potamachœrus*), and are invariably stained black.

The shield of the Kanemboo negroes in the army of the Sultan of Borneo is about 4 by 2 feet and of an oval shape.   It is of an extremely light wood, which grows in the shallow waters of Lake Tchad.   The pieces of which it is made are bound together with strips of raw-hide with the hair on.   These straps make a vandyked pattern across the shield and around its edge.   The Arab shield of Zanzibar[192] is round, 18 inches in diameter, made of rhinoceros hide, and worn at the back from the left shoulder.   The Abyssinian shield is made of buffalo hide, and its convex outer surface has a boss in the center.   It is ornamented with the mane,

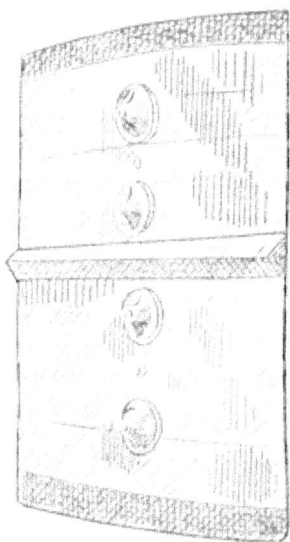

Fig. 126.—*Monbuttoo wooden shield, Central Africa.*

tail, and paw of a lion, if the owner has been so fortunate as to kill one ; others have silver or brass plates.   Around the shield are holes, through which passes the thong by which it is suspended.   It is changed so as to hang by a different hole each day, in order that it may not become warped.   The Nubian shield is made of hippopotamus or crocodile skin, and has a central projecting boss formed of a separate piece of skin.   It is stretched on a wooden frame-work.   The notches in its perimeter are a fashion, probably the remaining impression of some ancient shape.

The shields of ancient Asia Minor and Assyria and the modern shields of India show the various shapes and materials which we have cited. The large shield of the Assyrians, used at sieges, was of wicker-work or hide ; it had a curved point or a projection like a roof.   It was held by a shield bearer.[193]   The oblong standing shield was referred to by Herodotus, who said[194] "the Persians made a fence of their osier shields." The Assyrians had also circular bucklers of hide or metal.   The oval copper shield found by Dr. Schliemann in the excavations at Hissarlik,[195] 28 feet below the surface, is 20 inches in length, quite flat, except a raised rim and boss.   Herodotus says[196] that the Carians invented the handle of the shield, previous to which time it had been strung by a strap from the

[191] Smith's Dict., Gr. & Rom. Antiq., London, 1875, p. 1043.
[192] Ruschenberger's "Voyage Round the World," p. 54.
[193] Iliad, b. viii, l. 319, 327 ; 1 Samuel, xvii, 7 ; Layard's Nineveh, Pls. vii, viii.
[194] Herodotus, l. 9, c. 61.
[195] Schliemann's "Troy and its Remains," Pl. xiv, opp. p. 324.
[196] l. i, c. 171.

neck. The bucklers used during the Trojan war had wooden handles.[197]

One circular shield shown from India was of rhinoceros hide, 18 inches in diameter, and ornamented with circular plates of iron. The round buckler of the Kurds[198] and Arabs are made of the hide of the hippopotamus. The Lepcha[199] (Sikkim) shield is of cane with a tuft of yak hair in the middle. The ancient Singhalese[200] shields were sometimes covered with plates of the chank shell (*Turbinella rapa*). This is yet used as an ornament in some parts of Malaysia. It is a spiral shell,[201] the fishing for which is a monopoly on the Chinese coast, and is rented like the pearl fishery. The great market for the shells is in India, where they are sawed into rings, and worn by the Indian women on their arms, legs, toes, and fingers. In Bengal the shell has a ceremonial use, and is buried with opulent and distinguished persons.

The Malaysian shields[202] are usually of wood. Two were shown in the Netherlands colonies collection. Fig. 127 is strengthened against splitting by transverse strips of bamboo sewed on with ratan. The wood is half an inch thick, the shield 4 feet long and 18 inches wide. The other shield, Fig. 128, is also of wood, and belongs to the Dyaks of Borneo.[203] The shape is somewhat peculiar, being narrowed in the middle and pointed above and below. In the example, the wood has bindings of ratan and tufts of human hair set in the

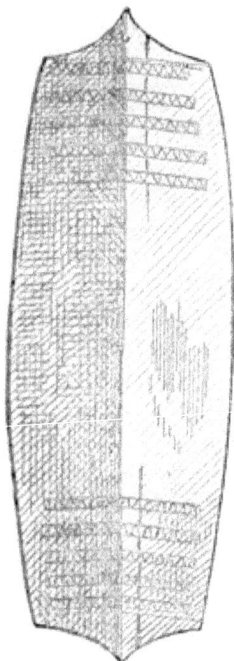

Fig. 127.—*Wooden shield of the Malays.*

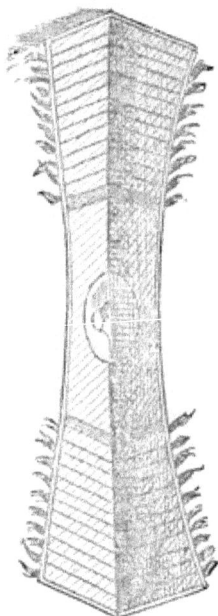

Fig. 128.—*Wooden shield, Dyaks of Borneo.*

Fig. 129.—*Leathern shield, Philippine Islands.*

[197] Iliad, viii, 193.
[198] "Nineveh," vol. ii, p. 266.
[199] Hooker's "Himalaya," vol. i, p. 301.
[200] Tennent's "Ceylon," vol. i, p. 500.
[201] Bertolacci's "Ceylon," 264.
[202] Raffle's "Java," 4to, i, Pl. opp. p. 276.
[203] Wood, vol. ii, pp. 475-76.

edges. It is 4 feet long, 10 inches at the widest and 6 inches at the midlength. Other shields have beads and feathers, either separately or with the tufts of hair. The plain wooden surfaces are sometimes painted with geometric figures.

The Philippine Islands collection had a number of shields—one of hide and a number of wood. Fig. 129 is a buckler of hide painted with geometric figures. Figs. 130 and 131 are four wooden shields of the Philippines. They are from 3 to 5 feet long and from 10 to 12 inches broad. They may also be classed among the parrying weapons, being evidently intended to glance off arrows or spear thrusts. The shield (*kalasag*) of the Ygorrotes of the Philippines is of wood covered on the edge with ratan, and is 19 inches in circumference.[204] The shield of the Malakus[205] of the Eastern Archipelago is narrow, of hard wood, bent to an arc shape, inlaid with bits of shell, and provided with a single handle placed in the center. The warriors of the Solomon Islands use clubs, spears, bows and arrows. Their oval shields are of rushes so thickly plaited as to resist arrows.

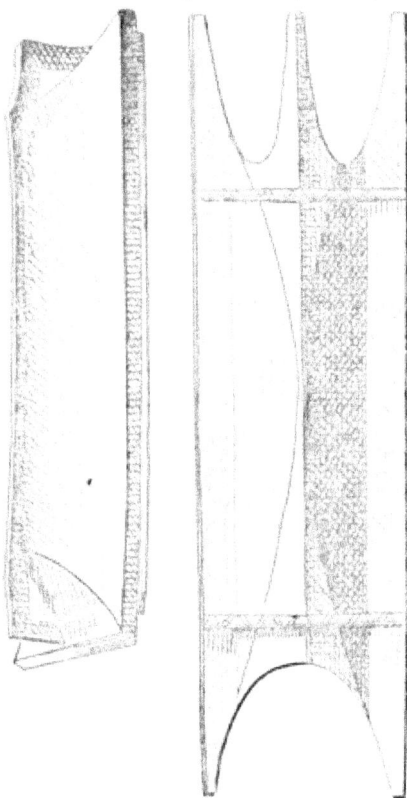

FIG. 130.— *Wooden shields, Philippines.*

The Siamese shield, Fig. 132, is indebted for its lightness, stiffness, and strength to the bamboo. It is 5 feet in height, 20 inches in width, and has two thicknesses of plaited bamboo splits, inclosing a layer of plantain or bamboo leaves.

The Chinese shield (Fig. 133) is made of ratan cane, coiled from the center outward, and interlaced with ratan splits proceeding in a general radial direction. The diameter is 32 inches, the height of the cone 8 inches. It has a cross-bar lashed by ratan splits and an arm-loop and hand-grasp similarly attached.

The Australian shields are of three general descriptions: The *towerang*, or *mulga* (Fig. 134), which is light, long, and narrow, used for warding off the blows of spears and boomerangs by a circular twist which deflects them from their course; the *heilamon* (*gee-am*) or oval shield, which covers the person more or less perfectly and receives the impact of the

[204] Jagar, "Philippines," p. 240.
[205] Belcher's "Eastern Archipelago," vol. ii, p. 376.

weapon; and a smaller shield held like a cricket-bat in the hand by a handle at the end. On this island continent are various tribes, with varying dialects, and the names of the shields are not the same in all districts. The names *mulga* and *gee-am* are those given by R. Brough Smith.[26]

The *towerang* (*mulga*) or parrying shield was shown in the Victoria section of the Australian department. It is 2½ or 3 feet long and used for fencing off the blows of missiles by striking them in flight.

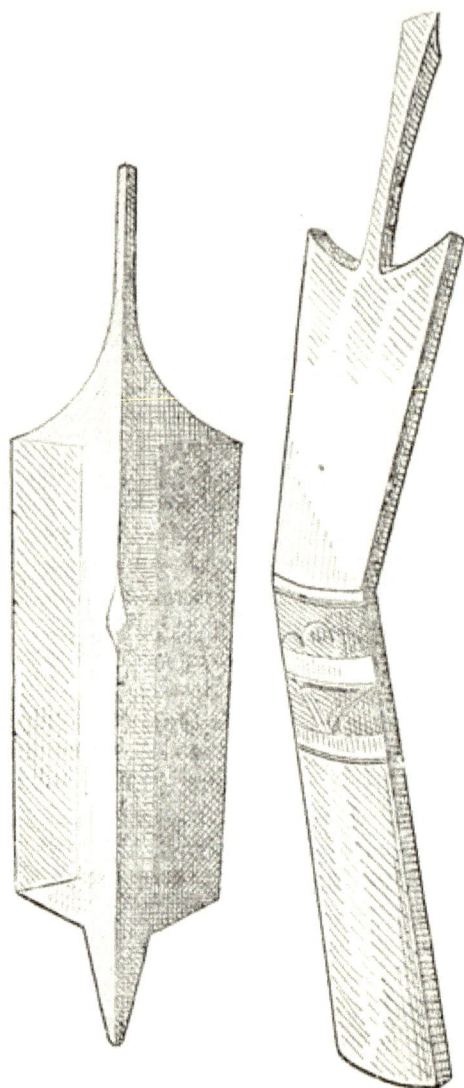

FIG. 131.—*Wooden shields of the Philippines.*

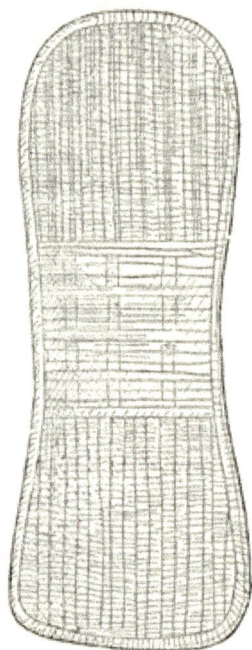

FIG. 132.—*Basket-work shield of Siam.*

It is made from the blue-gum tree, which is relatively hard and heavy, enabling it when it strikes a flying weapon to swerve it from its flight without too great a strain on the wrist. The hand-hold is cut out of the solid back of the shield, or, when the material is thin, the ends of the handle piece are driven through the front of the shield and secured.

The size given by R. Brough Smith is 35 by 5 inches, and he states that they are usually made of iron-wood or the box-wood of the colony.

[26] Aborigines of Victoria. Melbourne, 1878, pp. 330–334.

All have hand-holds, made out of the solid, and the weight is from $2\frac{1}{2}$ to $3\frac{1}{4}$ pounds. A variety of sizes and some variation of patterns are shown in Figs. 113–129 of his work.[25]

The *heilamon* (*gee-am*), or war shield, used by the aborigines of New South Wales, is 2 feet long, 10 inches broad, and usually made from a solid block of wood, though sometimes from bark. The depression and hand-grasp are carved out of the

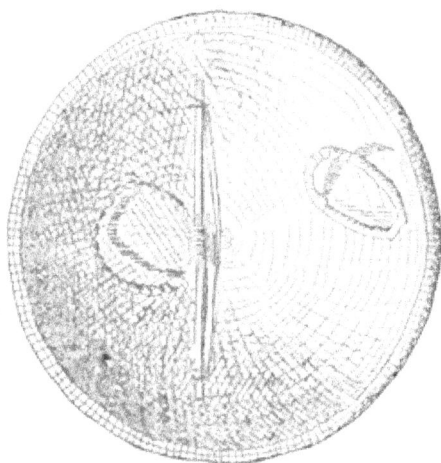

Fig. 133.—*Chinese shield of basket-work.* (*Inside.*)

wood. That shown in Fig. 135 is made from the wood of the gigantic nettle-tree. In other parts of Australia the bark of some one of the numerous species of gum is bent to form by the application of heat, and a handle or arm bow is lashed on. The shape is usually a long oval, but some are of a diamond shape. The bark shield is called *mulabakka*. The Murray River blacks make canoes, by means of this bending process, from the bark of the tea-tree (*melaleuca, i. e.,* black and white), and from various species of *eucalypti*.

In the work just referred to,[26] the larger shield, for general protection, is spoken of as generally made of green bark, which is curved by laying it upon an earthen mound of the required shape, covered with hot embers; the bark is laid thereon and weighted with stones. It has a hand-grasp of the original wood, or one is inserted. The size is 38 by 10 inches.

Fig. 134.—*Towerang or parrying shield of Australia.*

Fig. 135.—*Heilamon or war-shield of New South Wales.*

The Victoria section of the Australian department showed shields of

[25] Aborigines of Victoria, Melbourne, 1878, p. 300 *et seq.*

[26] *Ibid.*, p. 382, Figs. 131–139.

the third kind (Fig. 136), each having a handle, so that it looked like a bat. Such a shield is 24 by 10 inches, and is made by shrinking bark into a curved shape by water and heat and stiffening it with a cross stick.

The wooden shield of Western Australia is shown in Smith's work.[209]

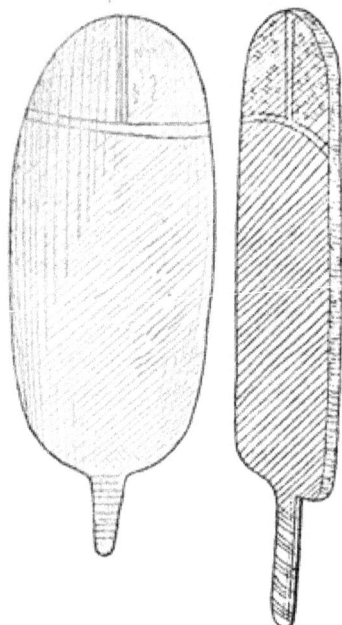

The shield of the North American Indian is made of buffalo hide. In making it, a piece of bull-buffalo skin is selected, twice as large as the shield required. A hole is dug in the ground, as large as the future shield, and a smudge of smoke of rotten wood is made under the skin, which is pegged above. As the skin is heated, a glue made of the horns and hoofs is rubbed in hot, which causes the skin to contract, and the pegs are regularly loosened to allow it to shrink, at the same time keeping it stretched. When it has imbibed the necessary quantity of glue, and has reached the dimensions of the hole, being twice as thick as in its natural condition, it is ready for the trimming and dressing which complete it as a shield

The Uaupé Indians of the Amazon[210] use shields of wicker-work, sometimes covered with tapir skin. Sometimes the hide of the raca marina or sea cow is used

Fig. 136.—Wooden shields of Victoria, Australia.

by the Amazon Indians for making shields; it is the largest animal accessible, and its skin fills the place occupied by the rhinoceros, hippopotamus, and elephant hide in the torrid regions of Africa.

VI.—BOWS AND ARROWS.

The use of poison upon arrows by savages is very ancient, and is yet found in many distant parts of the world. The very name for "poison" in Greek (toxicon)—and the Latin is similar—is derived from the word equivalent to "arrow." Commencing our notice of bows and arrows with South Africa, the first example we find is the poisoned arrow of the bosjesman, or bushman.[211]

> "But black as death, the thin-forged bitter point,
>   That with the worm's blood late did erst anoint."
>   Death of Paris.   (EARTHLY PARADISE.)

This arrow is in several pieces; the head is a triangular iron plate inserted into the end of a short section of reed, which slips over a piece

[209] Aborigines of Victoria, Melbourne, 1878, p. 239, Fig. 148.
[210] Wallace's "Amazon," p. 504.
[211] Casalis' Basutos, xiv; Livingstone's Travels, p. 189; Baine's South Africa, pp. 144, 159, 164.

ot ostrich-bone socket in the reed-shaft of the arrow. In some cases the weapon consists of as many as five parts; a piece of ivory on the end of the section of reed and holding the iron point, which is daubed with poison. In each case the glutinous poison holds the iron tip, and the latter comes off in the wound. The poison is either from the putrified cocoons of an insect, the 'kaa or ngwa, of Livingstone, from the poison gland of the puff-adder, or from the *Euphorbia arborescens.* The arrows are carried in a neat quiver of bark sewed with sinew. The bow and quiver are slipped into a small buck-skin, the neck of which is tightly bound round the bottom of the quiver, while the legs serve as belts to swing it over the shoulders. The quiver also contains the fire-stick and sucking-tube of the bushman.

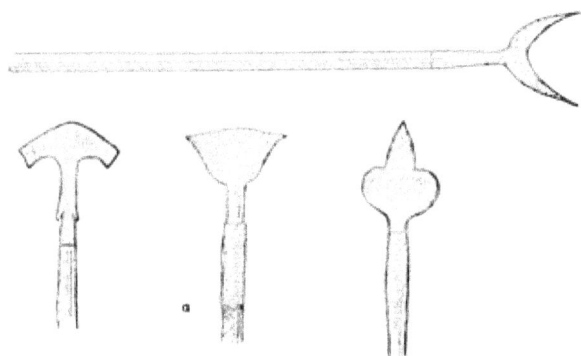

FIG. 137.—*Iron arrow-heads of Angola, Africa.*

The Kafir does not use the bow and arrow, although he suffers from the poisoned arrows of the bosjesman and fears their effects. The Kafir weapons are the assegai and kerrie; that is, javelin and club.

The Angola arrows, Fig. 137, have heads of steel on reed-shafts. The metal is obtained of very good quality by native methods. Their spear and javelin heads for thrusting and throwing are likewise tipped with steel. The arrow-heads shown in Fig. 137 are bound to the shafts with raw hide, grass, or ratan. The arrow-head (a) is like one form of the *bosjesman* arrow, in which the base of the triangular steel piece is in advance.

The poisoned arrows of the Zambesi[212] and Mozambique countries are made in two pieces, after the same general plan of those of the bushman of the south. The iron barb is fastened to a wand of wood 10 inches long, which slips into a reed shaft. The wood below the arrow-head is smeared with the poison, and both the barb and the stick remain in the wound while the reed drops off. The poison is obtained from a species of *strophanthus.* The bow of the Zambesi Maravi[213] is intended to act as a shield as well, being from 6 to 8 inches broad, and used in parrying thrusts.

A Central African quiver brought by Long Bey is shown in Fig. 138. Like that of the Gold Coast it is of wood bound with leather, and has tassels of the same. A sheathed knife is attached to the quiver. The Niam-niams,[214] on the extreme upper waters of the Nile, do not use the bow and arrow. The Monbuttoo,[215] immediately south of them, on the

[212] Livingstone's "Zambesi," pp. 109, 491.   [213] Schweinfurth's "Africa," vol. ii, p. 9.
[213] *Ibid.*, p. 583.   [215] *Ibid.*, vol. ii, pp. 103, 111.

Welle River, have both. The shafts of the Monbuttoo arrows are of reeds, and differ from all others of that vicinity in being winged with pieces of genet's skin or plantain leaves. The bows are over 3 feet long, and the strings made of a strip of the split Spanish reed, which possesses more elasticity than any cord. A hollow piece of wood on the bow protects the thumb from the blow of the string. The arrow is discharged from between the middle fingers. The Dinkas[236] of the Upper Nile have no bow and arrow; their weapons are lances and clubs. The Bongos[237] use the lance, bow, and arrow. Their bows are 4 feet long, the arrows 3 feet, made of solid wood, and anointed with the milky juice of *euphorbia*. The Madi and Bari[238] tribes of Central Africa also use

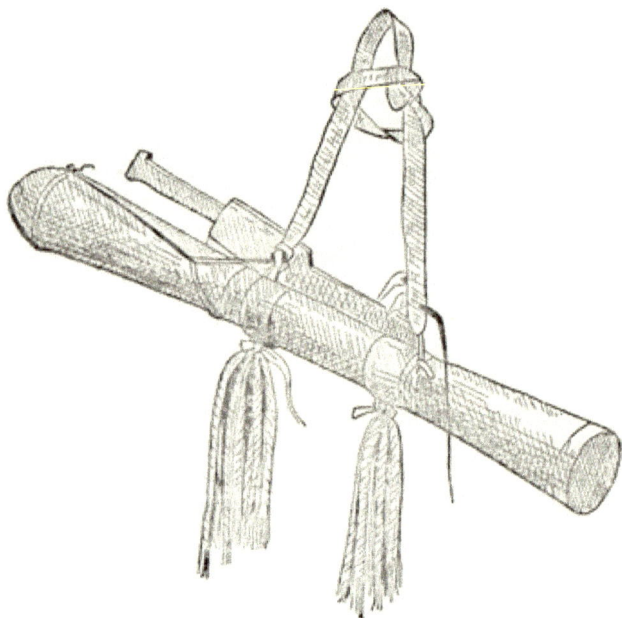

FIG. 138.—*Quiver of Uganda, Africa.*

poisoned arrows; so do the Ashantees, Fans, and Aponos of the West.

The modes of handling the bow in Africa are various, and have always been so. In ancient Egypt[239] several modes were adopted even by the trained troops. The mural monuments show a bowman with three supplementary arrows held by the thumb, the string being pulled to the shoulder by the fingers. An arrow being discharged another one is jerked up, and three are kept in the air at a time. Another figure shows a soldier drawing a longer bow, having a larger arrow, and pulling with the thumb and finger.

The Assyrians drew the bow to the cheek or to the ear, as did the Saxons—not to the breast like the Greeks. The larger Assyrian bow was carried over the shoulder, the man first putting his head through

[236] Schweinfurth's "Africa," vol. i, p. 154.   [238] Baker's "Ismailia," pl. opp. p. 135.
[237] Ibid., vol. ii, p. 300.   [239] Wilkinson; Kitto, vol. i, p. 452.

it. The smaller bow was carried in a quiver by the side of the chariot along with the arrows, which were reeds with heads of iron or copper. A linen guard was strapped to the inside of the left arm to protect the arm against the blows of the string.

The bow and arrow of Queensland, Australia, are shown in Fig. 139. The bow is 6 feet long and made of the male bamboo, which is solid. The string is a strip of ratan, which is beaten to remove the flinty coating and reduce it to a bunch of fibers, which is slightly twisted. The arrow is of reed, from 3 to 5 feet long, has no nick for the string, nor feathers for the butt. The arrow-head is of hard wood, smooth, knobbed, or barbed. As the bow and arrow are used only in the northerly part of Australia,[220] around the Gulf of Carpentaria and in Queensland, it may reasonably be assumed that they are of foreign origin, and the knowledge of them imported from Papua.

The New Guinean[221] arrow is a reed tipped with hard, heavy wood, grooved to receive a tapered slice of bamboo with a point made by an oblique cut. The arrow is poisoned. The bow is 6 feet in length, made from the cocoa-nut tree, and has a string of ratan. The arrows of the Solomon Islanders are tipped with fish-bones; those of the Admiralty Islands are of reed with hard-wood heads secured by ligatures of bark. The Tonga Island arrows are of reed and hard wood, the junction of the two being covered with plaited sinnet and varnished. The Andaman Islanders[222] use a bow of tough, strong wood 5 or 6 feet in length, and having two flat bulges, one on each side of the central hand-hold. The arrows are of ratan with a hard-wood head and a barb made of a fish-bone, the tail-bone of the sting-ray, or a nail when one can be procured. The point of the arrow is sometimes poisoned.

The bow of the Philippine Islands is a slab off the side of a large bamboo, or it is sometimes made of caryota wood; the string of abacá, 3ᵐᵐ in diameter.[223]

Other arrows (*pana*) have shafts (*gaho*) of caryota wood and points (*buchi*) of bamboo, or sometimes the whole arrow is of wood 1ᵐ to 1.8ᵐ in length. The heads are hastate, barbed, three-pointed, or carved spirally.

Fig. 139.—Australian bow (Queensland) made of bamboo.

[220] Wood, vol. ii, p. 46.

[221] *Ibid.*, vol. ii, p. 225.

[222] Mouat's "Andaman," pp. 271, 321.

[223] Jagor's "Travels in the Philippines," London, 1875, pp. 657, 138, 210.

They have different names: *bulóg, boló, scrápong,* &c. They are sometimes dipped in a poisonous mixture looking like tar, and made from the mixed inspissated juices obtained from the bark of two trees. The quiver is of bamboo; the arrow is frequently a cane with a tip of hard wood (sharpened), bamboo, bone, or metal. The arrows exhibited in the Spanish Building are shown in Fig. 140.

The bow, club, and sling are not found among the primitive Dyaks or any other aborigines of Malayo-Polynesia, except the Bisayan race.[224] The Sagais of Borneo use the *sumpitan*[225] for propelling poisoned arrows by means of the force of the breath. The natives called a rocket a "fire sumpitan." The blow-gun, which is similar to the *zarabatana* of the Macooshees[226] of South America, is a tube of hard wood (*Casuarina equisetifolia*), 7 or 8 feet long, and with a bore of half an inch. An iron muzzle-sight is fixed upon the upper side and a spear upon the lower, the latter serving to keep the tube straight, its projecting blade also serving as a weapon. The arrow,

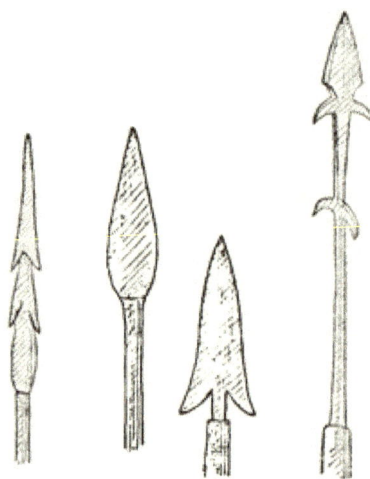

FIG. 140.—*Iron arrow-heads of the Philippines.* sumpit, is 9 inches in length, formed of a leaflet rib of the *nibon* palm. The point of hard wood is smeared with the deadly poison of the Upas tree, and has brittle barbs or the tail-bone of the sting-ray, which breaks off in the wound. The arrow is run through a cone of the pith of the *nibon* wood, which fits the bore and prevents windage. The range is variously stated at from 40 to 150 yards—from 40 to 80 yards is the more probable statement.

The common bow of India is made from the male bamboo, bound at intervals with belts of split ratan. Another form is made of horn and wood. The hand-hold and the ends are wood and the two intervening pieces are of a buffalo horn which is sawed lengthwise, flattened by heat and pressure, and fastened by long splice joints to the middle and end pieces. It is like the *arcus patulus* of the Romans. Sinews are laid along the back of the bow and so agglutinated by heat, moisture, and pressure that they appear to form one piece with the body of the bow. The whole is then anointed with *glue* and ornamented according to taste. The horn portions are principally involved in the flexure, and when the bow is unbent it recurves and assumes the shape of the letter "C," the back being inward like the *arcus sinuosus* of the classic period. The bow string is of vegetable fiber. The arrow is of reed with a hard-wood

[224] Belcher's "Eastern Archipelago," vol. ii, p. 338.
[225] Boyle's "Dyaks of Borneo," pp. 251, 252; Raffles' "Java," 4to, vol. i, p. 296, and Pl.; Belcher's "Eastern Archipelago," vol. i, p. 227; vol. ii, pp. 133, 134.
[226] Wood, vol. i, p. 583.

point and butt, the former receiving a quad-
rangular steel piece, and the latter the feathers
and the notch for the string. Another Indian
arrow has a wooden shaft with barbed head
lashed to the shaft with twine, and "feath-
ered," so to speak, with dry leaves set in slits
in the butt of the arrow.

The maritime people of Ceylon are largely
from the Malabar coast of India and are dis-
tinct both from the Singhalese, the principal
nation of the island, and from the Veddahs,
the wild aborigines who still inhabit the less
accessible forests. The Singhalese chronicles
record that the Malabar arrows were sometimes "drenched with the poison of serpents."[227]

The Veddahs[228] are expert with the bow,
which they hold in the right hand and draw
the string with the left. The bow is 6 feet
long, and the arrow 3 feet.[229] Iron arrow
blades[230] are the only articles of foreign manufacture which they covet. Another Veddah
bow is sprung by the feet,[231] the string being
held by both hands, the archer lying upon his
back. This unusual mode is mentioned by Ar-
rian,[232] and is practiced by the *Cabaclos* of Brazil[233] and the *Gran Chacos* of La Plata.

The Tartars and Chinese use a bow which
assumes a recurved form when unstrung. The
example shown in Fig. 141 was upon the effigy
of a Chinese soldier in the Mineral Annex to the
Main Building. It is nearly 6 feet in length
and a few inches from each end is a bone stud
over which the string passes. The bow is
bent by placing it behind the right thigh and
in front of the left, then bending it by a sud-
den stoop of the body throwing the force on
the right leg, and, by a quick motion, catching
the string over the end of the bow and into the
notch. The body of the bow is a bent bamboo
strip of the solid variety, and to its ends
wooden pieces are lashed with sinews. It has
a cord string. The shape is exactly that of the
Scythian bow (*arcus scythicus*) as shown on

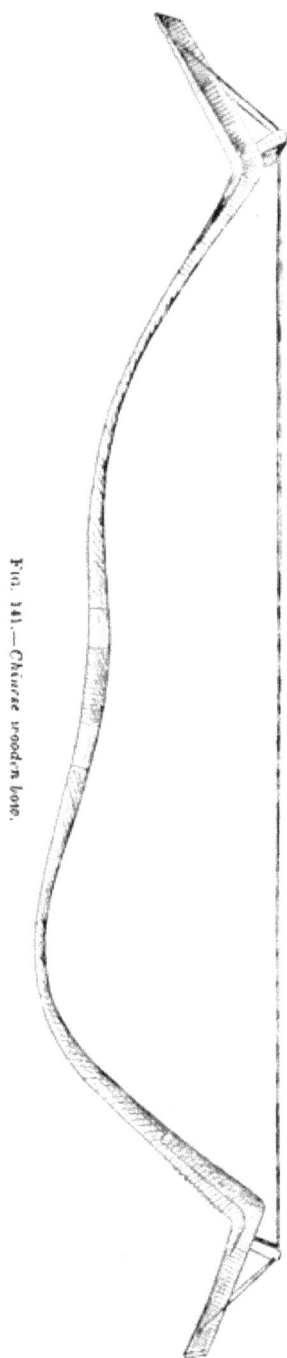

FIG. 141.—*Chinese wooden bow.*

[227] Tennent's "Ceylon," vol. i, p. 500.
[228] Knox, "Ceylon," 61.
[229] H. S., "Ceylon," London, 1876, vol. i.
[230] Forbes' "Ceylon," vol. ii, p. 78.
[231] Tennent's "Ceylon," vol. i, p. 499.
[232] Indica, l. xvi
[233] Fletcher & Kidder's "Brazil," p. 558.

classic vases and gems. The Japanese bows and arrows are shown in Siebold's great work.[211]

The bow of the North American Indian is seldom much over 4 feet long and is always used on horseback; his aim is not remarkable for accuracy, but he discharges the arrows with great force and rapidity. The bow is made of wood, bone, or iron. An ash bow with the sinews of the buffalo or deer worked into the back is no contemptible weapon either to draw or to face. The bow, Fig. 142, like the Roman *arcus patulus*, is made of several horns spliced together. In the present case, the horns are those of the mountain sheep, *Ovis Montana*. They are made by heating the horns in hot ashes and drawing them out, then splicing pieces together with bands of deer sinew. The joints are hidden by ornamental coverings of cloth, skin, or dyed porcupine quills. Such bows are valued at the price of two horses, as the horns of which they are made must be obtained by barter with Rocky Mountain Indians. The arrow is of wood or reed and headed with flint, bone, or iron. Indian arrow-heads are the most common article in the American sections of ethnological museums, and show wide difference in shape, material, and size. The example, Fig. 143, has a point of chipped chalcedony. Fig. 144 also shows chipped flint arrow-heads of the Pai-Utes of Southern Utah. They are cemented and bound to the wooden shafts.

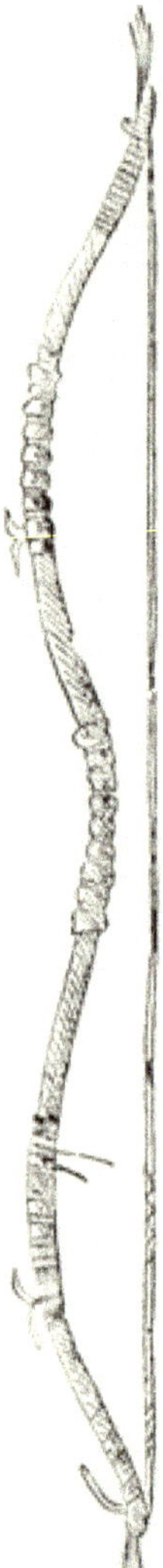

The Indians of the California peninsula make bows of willow-root, and attach strings of intestines. Their arrows are of reed with triangular hard-wood heads.[215] Flint arrowheads of Terra del Fuego, and of the stone age of Sweden, are shown and described in Nilson,[236] and those of the dwellers on the pile villages of the Swiss lakes, in Desor's work.[217] Bone arrow points and bows of yew are also found in the same localities.[218]

Fig. 142.—*Sioux Indian bow of mountain sheep's horns.*

Fig. 143.—*Sioux stone-pointed arrow. Dakota.*

[211] "Nippon," vi, Pl. 1, *bis*; vii, Pl. 19, Figs. 1, 1, *a*, 2; vi, Pl. 22; see also *Ibid.* ii, Pl. 5, for bows and arrows in great variety. Also upper row in Pl. 15 and 21, vol. ii.
[215] Baegart, in Smithsonian Report., 1863, pp. 362, 3.
[236] Stone age, Plate v. and pages i, 43-5.
[217] Translation in Smithsonian Report, 1865, p. 374, 356.
[218] Morlot. Translation in Smithsonian Report, 1862, p. 376.

The Oregon Indians make their bows of cypress, *Cupressus Lawsoniana*, or of yew, *Taxus brevifolia*. The wood is strengthened on the back with sinew, in the manner so common throughout the Northwest. The string is of sinew and the arrow of reed pointed with obsidian. The arrow-head is chipped to form by a tool similar to that by which the glazier nibbles his glass to shape. The feathers of the arrow are set on spirally. Poison for the arrow-heads is made by causing a rattlesnake to strike its fangs into liver, which is then allowed to putrify and the arrows are smeared therewith. The bow of the Ahts of Vancouver's Island [239]

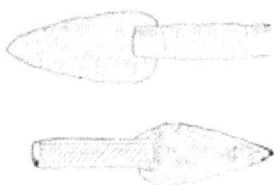

FIG. 144.—*Chipped flint arrow-heads, Utah.*

is also of wood fortified with sinews. The arrow is large and has a barbed bone lip; the arrow for fish has two tips barbed on the inside like the Australian fishing-spear, and clasps any object it may come across. The feathering of the arrow is put on spirally. The Ahts have also an arrow with a detachable barbed bone point, connected by two cords with the shaft, with which they form an equilateral triangle: the shaft impedes the seal in its motions and acts as a float. The same feature is common in Eskimo harpoons.

The bow of the Kutchin tribes of the Mackenzie and Youcon Rivers are of willow, 5 feet long and with an enlargement at the grasp to protect the hand against the snap of the string. The arrows are of pine: arrow-head of bone of wild-fowl, or of bone tipped with iron for moose or deer. [240]

The bow of the Greenland Eskimo is made of horn, bone, or wood, re-enforced on the outer side with a multitude of deer sinews, which are put on so tight as to give the bow some backward curvature. Its average length is 3½ feet. The bow string is twisted deer sinews. The Eskimo arrows are of wood tipped with bone or stone; or in some cases of wood and bone tipped with iron. Bow and arrows are in a quiver of seal-skin. Fig. 145 shows three arrow-heads in the Greenland division of the Danish department; the left-hand is of bone and the others of stone. The Eskimo uses a wrist-guard of bone plates tied together and fastened by a button and loop; it receives the blow of the bow-string.

In the warmer regions of America, like the countries to which we have referred, the poisoned arrow is no new thing. Herrera, the Spanish adventurer, died from the

FIG. 145.—*Eskimo arrows, Greenland.*

effects of a poisoned arrow. De Soto's historians [241] mention arrows barbed with flint, arrows without barbs, arrows of reed tipped with

[239] Wood, vol. ii, p. 725.   [240] Smithsonian Report, 1866, p. 322.
[241] Irving, op. cit., pp. 191, 195, 225.

lozenge-shaped buck's-horn plates, and arrows tipped with fish-bones, with palm spikes, and with hard wood.

The *zarabatana*[242] or blow-gun of the Guiana tribes is made in two pieces, each of which has a semi-cylindrical groove, so that the two form a perfect tube when bound together with spiral strips of the pliable *incitara* wood. The outside is covered with wax and resin. A trumpet-shaped mouth-piece directs the wind from the mouth and lungs into the tube when the lips are suddenly opened; the puff seems to be directly from the chest. The blow-gun is 12 feet long and quite heavy. A lighter gun, *pucuna*, of the same region, is made of a ten or fifteen feet section of a reed (*Arundinaria Schombergii*), which grows in a limited region on the Upper Orinoco, and has a length of over 12 feet between the joints of its lower portion. This reed forms the *ourah* or barrel and is slipped into a stick of palm (*Ircartia setigera*) from which the pith has been pushed out. The mouth-piece end is bound with silk grass and the other end fortified with the half of an *acuero* nut, which also forms the muzzle sight. The breech sight is made of two incisor teeth of a cavy, which are secured with wax to the tube, the depression between the teeth being the valley sight. The gun is held in the left hand, the elbow of that arm resting on the hip. The right hand grasps the tube near the mouth piece, and the gun is raised by bending the body. It weighs about a pound and a half—but a fraction of the weight of the *zarabatana*. The arrow is made of the leaf rib of the *concourite* palm. It is 10 inches in length, about the size of a crow-quill, is pointed by means of a fish-tooth scraper, and is fitted to the bore with a pledget of wild cotton (*Bombax ceiba*). The arrows depend, like the *sumpits* of the Dyaks, upon their sharp poisoned tips. The poison is obtained from the *wourali* vine (*Strychnos toxifera*) and a bitter root, the *hyarri*, to which are added poisonous ants, poison fangs of snakes, and other things to give effect to the stuff, or to conceal the real ingredients, as the composition is a secret in the hands of the conjuror. The poison has an instantaneous numbing effect, the victim seeming void of pain or fear, dropping immediately, and dying in a short time without a struggle. The arrows are kept in a "quiver" or in a "roll," and each is cut deeply near the head, so that the poisoned portion may break off in the wound. The range is from 50 to 100 yards. A modification of the arrow is one in which, instead of the cotton, a piece of bark is placed spirally on the stem of the arrow, terminating in a hollow cone, which fills the bore when the cone is expanded by the wind; a singular anticipation of the hollow-base Minie bullet, which is expanded into the grooves of the rifle by the evolution of gases due to the explosion of the powder. A piece or two of bark, laid spirally on the arrow-shaft, feather the arrow, and make it revolve in flying. This is equivalent to the rifling of a gun. This arrow is tipped with a small piece of iron.

For war or for killing the tapir or jaguar, an arrow 6 feet long is made of a reed, having for a head a hard-wood spike, an iron point, or the tail bone of the sting-ray. Poison is used on either. The arrow is projected by a bow.

The blow-gun of the Uaupés of the Amazon[242] is called the *grava-tana*, and is made of two stems of the small palm *Ireartia setigera*, one slipping within the other so as mutually to correct curvatures. The pith is pushed out, and a conical mouth-piece fitted to one end. Arrows are made from the spinous processes of the *patawa* (*Œnocarpus batawa*), pointed and anointed with poison of the *woorali*. The butt of the arrow carries a little tuft of tree cotton to make it fit in the tube.

The ordinary bow of the Uaupés,[243] the aboriginal Indians of Brazil, is of different kinds of hard elastic wood, and is from 5 to 6 feet long. The string is either of the *tucum* leaf-fiber (*Astrocaryum vulgare*), or the inner bark of trees called *tururi*. The arrows are 5 feet long or over, are made of the flower-stalk of the arrow-grass, and are tipped with hard wood, barbed with the serrated spine of the sting-ray. For war, the head is anointed with poison, and is notched in two or three places so as to break off in the wound. Arrows for shooting fish have usually iron heads, bought of the traders, but others are made of monkey's bones and barbed. The arrows have three feathers laid on spirally.

The Indians of the Amazon also use a two-stringed bow for shooting stones. The pellet bow has a pad or net in the middle of the string, to hold a stone or ball of clay, to project it in the manner of an arrow. Such are used in South America and Africa.[244]

The arrow of the Guianians, used in shooting turtles, is projected by a bow and has a movable harpoon-head of iron detachable from the shaft, but secured loosely thereto by a thong. The turtle-shooting bow of the Central American Indians is made from the Soupar palm, *Guilielma speciosa*; the shafts of the arrows from the dry stalks of the cane, *saccharinum officinarum*, tipped with hard wood or iron.

The Peruvian arrows were tipped with copper or bone.[245]

The arrows of the Paraguayan Indians are of several kinds. Some have block points to kill birds without bleeding them; others with long wooden four-sided heads, sharpened and cut into barbs. These heads are carefully lashed on to the shaft, which is in all cases of cane. The arrows were shown in the Agricultural Building, are from 3 to 4 feet long, and have feather flyers put on straight.

The Gran Chaco Indian of the La Plata region,[246] destitute of habitation himself, employs fire-arrows when attacking a settlement. He binds some cotton around the head of each arrow just behind the head, and then lying down he holds the large bow with his feet while he draws the

[242] Wallace's Amazon, pp. 214, 215.
[243] *Ibid.*, pp. 486, 487.
[244] See Tylor's " Early History of Mankind," notes, p. 177.
[245] "Conquest of Peru," p. 73.
[246] Wood, vol. ii, p. 570.

string with both hands and lets fly the lighted arrows one after the other, with considerable rapidity. The *malleolus* of the Romans was a large missile like a distaff with an arrow-point; the cage of the distaff was filled with tow steeped in pitch. It was lighted before being discharged, and it was intended that the arrow should penetrate the wooden object or thatch and hold it while the incendiary material should set fire to the building.

The Fuegian bow is strung with twisted sinews; the arrow is of hard wood and has a notch in the end, holding a piece of flint or obsidian, which comes off in the wound.

We may conclude this account of savage weapons by some references to the cross-bow. This was shown in the Norwegian Department in the Main Building, and is a remnant of me-

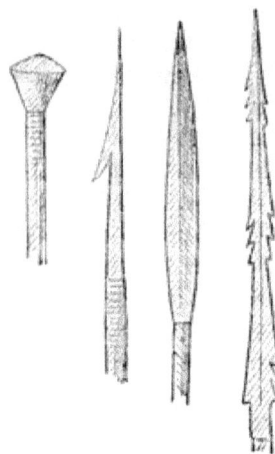

FIG. 146.—*Paraguayan arrows.*

diæval times. The instrument, however, is found in use in several parts of the world, and some of the African and Asiatic examples show more ingenuity than the European weapons with which we are more familiar.

The Norwegian cross-bow, Fig. 147, has a stock 30 inches long with a 24-inch powerful steel bow. The stock is handsomely inlaid with ivory; the string is a covered cord, and the bolt is shown in its groove. The Roman *scorpio* was perhaps the oldest instrument of the kind on record, and was used to discharge stones, plummets, and arrows. We find cross-bows among the Fans of the Gaboons in Western Africa; the Mishmi, a tribe of Assam

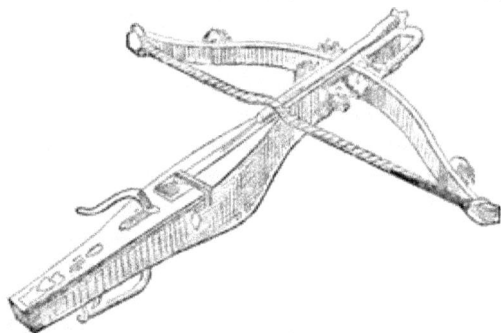

FIG. 147.—*Norwegian cross-bow.*

in Eastern India; the Nicobar Islanders[28]; the Chinese and the Japanese[29].

The cross-bow of the Fans is 5 feet long and has a very strong bow 2 feet long, which is bent by holding it with the feet while both hands strain the string into the notch. The string is thrust out of the notch by a clumsily ingenious arrangement. The shaft is split so that the forward end of the lower portion has a limited motion up and down, the split terminating at a point a little forward of the string-notch. To the lower portion is attached a peg which extends upward through a hole to thrust the string out of the notch. A trigger-pin lies in the split of the shaft and holds the portions apart so that the string can lie in the

[28] Wood, vol. ii, p. 220.   [29] Siebold's "Nippon," vol. ii, Pl. 5 bis.

notch; but as soon as the trigger-pin is removed the separated portions fly together, the pin rises, lifts the string, and the arrow is discharged. The Chinese have a somewhat similar method. The arrows of the Fan cross-bow are small and light, and about a foot in length. Their range is about 20 yards, and they owe their efficiency to their poisoned tips. When laid in the groove of the shaft to be discharged, the arrow is slightly held by a piece of wax. A larger arrow with an iron head is used in hunting.

The Japanese have also a cross-bow. The repeating Chinese cross-bow is perhaps the greatest advance in this implement, which has been so entirely superseded in Europe. The magazine is above a movable block which has a slot in which the string moves, and the whole block is movable back and forth in the main stock by a lever attached to the latter and shackled to the block. As the lever is raised the block slides forward until the string of the unbent bow drops into a notch. This allows an arrow to fall out of the magazine into the slot. Now draw back the lever; this action draws upon the bow-string and bends the bow in the first place, and when the lever is depressed to its fullest extent a pin in the block comes against the stock and is pushed up so as to lift the string out of the notch and discharge the arrow. The limit of speed in firing is the quickness with which the lever is lifted and depressed. The bow is made of three thicknesses of the male bamboo, overlapping like the plates of an elliptic carriage spring. The string is a thick twisted gut. The arrows are straight, both with heavy steel heads and very slight spiral feathers. Its utmost range is possibly 200 yards.

646388

www.ingramcontent.com/pod-product-compliance
Lightning Source LLC
Chambersburg PA
CBHW020303090426
42735CB00009B/1202